ON A NIGHT LIKE THIS

ON A NIGHT LIKE THIS

by John Godber

JOSEF WEINBERGER PLAYS

LONDON

JOHN GODBER

One of the most performed writers in the English language, John Godber was born in Yorkshire in 1956. A trained teacher with an MA in drama, it was whilst teaching from 1981-83 that he gained national recognition, winning major awards at the National Student Drama Festival and Fringe Firsts at the Edinburgh Festival. In 1984 he was appointed artistic director of Hull Truck Theatre Company. He has written over forty stage plays including *Bouncers, September in the Rain, Happy Jack, Up 'n' Under, Blood, Sweat and Tears, Teechers, Salt of the Earth, Cramp, Happy Families, Gym and Tonic, It Started With a Kiss, Passion Killers, Unleashed, Thick as a Brick, April in Paris, Lucky Sods, On the Piste,* and *The Office Party.*

With Jane Thornton he has co-written *Shakers* and an adaptation of Bram Stoker's *Dracula*. He has also written extensively for television including *Crown Court, Grange Hill* and *Brookside*, the six part BBC series *The Ritz* and its sequel *The Continental*, the screenplay *My Kingdom For A Horse* and the film of *Up 'n' Under*. John also devised the BBC series *Chalkface*, and has written the sports documentary *Body and Soul* for Channel Four Television.

ON A NIGHT LIKE THIS
First published in 2002
by Josef Weinberger Ltd
12-14 Mortimer Street, London, W1T 3JJ

ISBN 0 85676 260 1

Printed by Watkiss Studios Ltd, Biggleswade, Beds

ON A NIGHT LIKE THIS was first presented by Hull Truck Theatre Company on 7th December 2000 at the Spring Street Theatre, Hull, with the following cast:

RICHARD	James Hornsby
BECKY	Gillian Jephcott
SOPHIE	Hannah McBride
LEO	Rob Angell
DANNY	Nick Lane
VICKY	Hannah McBride
VAL	Gillian Jephcott
CARRIE	Hannah McBride
WAITER 1	Hannah McBride
WAITER 2	Nick Lane

Directed by John Godber
Designed by Ruth Paton

CHARACTERS

RICHARD JACKSON	Artist, 45
BECKY JACKSON	Marketing Consultant, 40
SOPHIE JACKSON	Their daughter, a student, 18
LEO HARDY	Decorator, 45
DANNY HARDY	Decorator, 30
VICKY HARDY	Danny's Wife, 24
VAL HARDY	Leo's Wife, 40
CARRIE	Prostitute, 24
FIRST WAITER	
SECOND WAITER	

ACTONE

Scene One

House. 8.10 am.

We are in the kitchen and dining room of a reasonably expensive house. The stage is covered with dustsheets, old and new cans of paint, a number of ladders of different shapes and sizes, and a number of planks for the higher areas. As the audience enter strains of classical music can be heard. When the house lights fade to black, the classical music fades to silence. LEO HARDY, *a sullen and dangerous but totally relaxed man in his mid-forties, enters. He is a painter and decorator, and is dressed accordingly. He brings with him a number of brushes and a large CD recorder, which is totally covered with splashes of paint.* LEO *looks at the job in hand, wipes a number of walls and considers a number of emulsion brushes and rollers. As he does this he chews heavily. He then walks over to the CD player and switches it on.* My Man, A Sweet Man, *plays. First* LEO *plays the music low, then he returns to the CD player and turns the music up significantly. He chews and listens to the music. He starts to pick up the beat. As he does this,* DANNY HARDY, *a thin man in his early thirties, enters. He too carries paint and associated articles. He doesn't take any notice of his cousin moving to the beat, and starts to paint himself.* LEO *picks up the beat and begins to dance with some style. Now one man is dancing and the other is painting. Slowly* DANNY *also starts to dance. The two men dance out what is clearly a well worked-out routine. They sing to the music doing the backing track and the main lyrics. Both men are dancing in a particular Northern Soul style. As they do this,* RICH JACKSON, *a bedraggled and educated looking man in his mid-forties wearing a pair of shorts and a T-shirt enters. He is barely awake. He watches as the two men dance.* LEO *and* DANNY *spot* RICH *but they do not stop their dance routine. In fact they go out of their way to acknowledge him as they dance. The two workmen continue to dance.* RICH *looks on bemused.* LEO *stops dancing and switches the music off. They are embarrassed.*

LEO   What's up?

RICH	Bloody hell!
LEO	What?
	(*There is immediate tension.*)
RICH	Can you keep it down a bit?
LEO	Oh, right!
RICH	I mean come on . . .
LEO	Yes, right.
RICH	Give us a break . . .
LEO	Who are you then?
RICH	I'm Richard Jackson. This is my house.
LEO	Oh, right.
RICH	Who are you?
LEO	I'm Leo, this is our Danny.
DANNY	(*still working*) All right?
	(*A beat.*)
LEO	We were just getting in the mood.
RICH	For what?
	(RICH *turns and makes to go back to bed.*)
LEO	Only Becky said to start as soon as we could.
RICH	Did she?
LEO	It is Becky, isn't it?
RICH	That's right.
LEO	I was going to say. I thought we'd come to 't wrong house for a minute!
RICH	No, we were expecting you, but –

LEO	Your wife then?
RICH	That's right.
LEO	Posh, isn't she?
RICH	Well, anyway . . .
LEO	I mean the way she talks like –
RICH	I'll let you get on then . . . but if you could just keep it down a bit . . .

(RICH *makes his way to exit, he has to fight his way past ladders and paint cans.* LEO *and* DANNY *watch in silence as he goes off.*)

| LEO | Put another track on Dan. |

(DANNY *moves to the CD player,* LEO *continues painting.*)

DANNY	"House for Sale?"
LEO	(*lyrics*) Milly Jackson . . .
DANNY	There's a house for sale. And I'm moving out today . . .
LEO	. . . It's got a spacious living room.
DANNY	. . . Just right for a bride and groom.

(DANNY *selects the track and switches it on.*)

| LEO | Turn it up a bit! |

(DANNY *turns the music back up to full, and returns to his job. Again as if by a process of distillation the music takes hold of the two of them and they begin to sing and dance. As they do* RICH *enters, he rubs his eyes in disbelief and watches them dancing.*)

| RICH | Hey bloody hell, come on! |

(*They ignore him, and continue to work.*)

LEO   You what?

               (RICH *is resigned to this encroachment and
               exits. The music swells as the lights fade.
               Blackout.*)

                        Scene Two

8.30 am.

DANNY *and* LEO *are still preparing the walls and busying
themselves with their work.*

LEO   Put it on again!

DANNY   (*sees* SOPHIE, *off*) Look out!

               (RICHARD'S *daughter* SOPHIE *enters. She is a
               young attractive nineteen year old. She is
               wearing revealing nightwear.*)

SOPHIE   (*yawning*) What's going on down here?

LEO   Morning.

DANNY   Morning.

SOPHIE   Morning.

DANNY   Oh . . . ah.

LEO   A pint of Guinness.

DANNY   A glass of milk.

SOPHIE   What are you on about?

DANNY   Morning.

LEO   Morning.

               (LEO *and* DANNY *laugh at* SOPHIE'S *expense.
               She looks around at all the mess.*)

SOPHIE   What's happened to the phone line upstairs?

LEO	He took a wire down when we were getting the ladders off the van. The one in here should work.
SOPHIE	Is the water still on?
LEO	Should be.
SOPHIE	(*yawning*) I'll make myself a cuppa then . . .
LEO	Two sugars in mine!
DANNY	Four in mine. No milk!
LEO	Who are you?
SOPHIE	I'm Sophie.
LEO	I'm a pint of Guinness.
DANNY	I'm a pint of milk.
	(SOPHIE *picks her way through the debris.*)
SOPHIE	(*half asleep*) I don't think we've got any Guinness!
LEO	Eh?
SOPHIE	Any Guinness?
LEO	That's a shame then!
SOPHIE	No, I . . .
LEO	Just a joke, cock . . .
SOPHIE	It's too early . . .
LEO	It's never too early, is it?
DANNY	Not for me!
	(*A beat.*)
SOPHIE	So are you going to tell me?

LEO	What?
SOPHIE	What the joke is!
LEO	Shall we?
DANNY	Will she get it?
LEO	I don't know!
SOPHIE	What is it? Something awful?
LEO	It's not that awful . . .
SOPHIE	What is it then?
LEO	Well when we see a woman we have to say how much we'd have to drink to sleep with her!
SOPHIE	Funny joke!
DANNY	I thought so!
LEO	Not so awful is it?
SOPHIE	Erm . . . yes!
DANNY	Hey, don't knock it kid.
SOPHIE	This is my home if you don't mind!
DANNY	Well you did quite well on your home turf. You were a glass of milk and a pint of Guinness. That's not bad. I mean Madonna's only a Diet Coke and a brandy isn't she?
SOPHIE	And I'm supposed to be flattered?
LEO	It could have been worse – we've just done a job where the daughter was three pints of scotch and a gas mask for me!
DANNY	Aye, and two shots of pethidine for me!
SOPHIE	Yes, but what does it say . . .
LEO	About who?

SOPHIE	About you?
LEO	It's only a joke . . .
SOPHIE	It's not, it's awful.
DANNY	It'd be awful if you had to sleep with her!
LEO	Why, do you think women don't do the same?
SOPHIE	Well I don't!
LEO	Come off it, you mean to tell me that you don't look at Brad Pitt and think it'd only take a mineral water and a hot dog?
SOPHIE	No.
DANNY	Our lass does, I think she'd even skip the hot dog!
LEO	You could do the same with us you know. I mean I'm probably a half of bitter, and our Danny's fifteen pints of Fosters and a bag of arsenic.
DANNY	Bollocks, you sarcastic git!
LEO	So go on, then . . .
SOPHIE	What?
LEO	What would it take?
SOPHIE	Oh, it's too early . . .
LEO	Give over . . .
	(RICH *has entered, and has been watching the action.* LEO *and* DANNY *have been unaware.*)
RICH	How are we doing?
SOPHIE	(*surprised*) Hi!
LEO	Can I use your loo, mate?
RICH	Just through the . . .

(LEO *moves close to her, and nods off stage.*)

LEO Any chance of getting that drink?

DANNY Yes, come on here, shape yourself!

LEO Down here, is it?

(LEO *exits.* DANNY *has collected a number of paint lids.*)

DANNY Where's your bin, Richard . . . ?

RICH Out through the conservatory.

DANNY Where's your bin? Do you get it? Dump this shit before it gets all over.

(DANNY *exits.* RICH *looks at* SOPHIE.)

RICH Sophe?

SOPHIE What?

RICH What are you doing?

SOPHIE They want a drink making.

RICH Well put some clothes on!

SOPHIE I didn't even know there was anybody here! Nobody ever tells me anything.

(DANNY *re-enters, as an after-thought.*)

DANNY Just to remind you – four sugars in mine and no milk, all right cock?

(*Music. Blackout.*)

Scene Three

9.15 am.

Silence. As the lights rise, DANNY *and* LEO *are sat on stage drinking from large cups.* RICHARD'S *wife* BECKY *enters. She is a very attractive, and likable woman who has just turned forty. She is dressed smartly and looking for some things in her briefcase. She has her car keys and a raincoat with her.* DANNY *reads a tabloid newspaper.*

BECKY   Is everything all right?

LEO   Just about . . .

BECKY   Up and at it this morning, weren't you?

LEO   Like to get a good start.

DANNY   Yeh, we like to get up while we're still half asleep, then we get more done before we waken up!

BECKY   You know where everything is, do you?

LEO   Don't worry, we'll find it if we need it!

DANNY   Lovely house . . .

BECKY   Well there's a lot of very valuable, erm . . .

LEO   Oh aye, you can see that.

DANNY   Don't worry about that. We'll take good care of that.

BECKY   That's good then.

DANNY   Oh aye, we'll have some of that.

BECKY   Sorry?

DANNY   I'm only kidding. Look at her face? She knows that, don't you?

BECKY   Well you never . . .

DANNY   I'm only kidding. I wouldn't nick 'owt. I'd tell me mates, though . . .

BECKY   Sorry?

DANNY   No honest I'm only Joking . . .

(*A beat.*)

BECKY   So how long do you think it'll . . . ?

LEO   I dunno, six weeks . . . ?

BECKY   Really?

LEO   Oh aye, now I've seen it . . . I mean we won't
            hang about, but doing a whole house this size,
            is a big 'un . . .

BECKY   Oh, well I'm away this weekend so . . . it's all
            yours . . .

LEO   Business or pleasure?

            (BECKY *is busy putting her briefcase together.*)

BECKY   A little bit of both really. There's a college
            reunion down in Bath! I haven't seen anybody
            for years, so . . . it's a bit of pressing the flesh.
            Poor Rich is going be here by himself, because
            Sophie's going to a concert.

LEO   It's all go for some!

BECKY   I dare say she'll be out of her head all weekend
            and Rich'll be bored out of his!

DANNY   What's he do, then?

BECKY   He paints.

DANNY   Like us!

BECKY   That's right!

LEO   Could have done all this himself then?

BECKY   He's a bit surreal for a dining room.

DANNY   What's he into? Women with three tits and
            stuff like that?

BECKY   Not far off!

LEO	Just like us then!
DANNY	Aye, I'm into all that, the more tits the better!
LEO	Well there's a spare brush there if he wants to help!
BECKY	(*hassled*) I'd better make a move. Is there anything else you want before I go?
LEO	Now there's an offer!
DANNY	That's rate!
LEO	Best offer we've had all week!
BECKY	Well, you must be desperate.
LEO	Hey, some of them are worth considering.
BECKY	Are they?
	(DANNY *puts down his paper and makes to exit for the toilet.*)
LEO	Oh aye . . . we get some offers.
DANNY	Well, he does . . .
LEO	You wouldn't know what to do Danny!
DANNY	'Course I would, it's like riding a bike.
LEO	Tha' never had a bike!
DANNY	I did, I had one with ape hangers on! Where's the bog did you say . . . ?
BECKY	At the bottom of the . . . I mean feel free to . . .
DANNY	I'll just, er . . .
	(DANNY *moves to exit.*)
LEO	Oh aye, we get some offers.
BECKY	Do you?

LEO   You'd be surprised!

BECKY   Would I?

LEO   Maybe you wouldn't, it depends what kind
           of life you live.

BECKY   Really?

LEO   Well you know what these big houses are like –
           there's a lot of stuff going off that we don't get
           to know about.

BECKY   Do you reckon?

LEO   Until it's in the papers.

BECKY   Well there's not much going off in this house
           that'll get in the paper.

LEO   You're the odd one out in this street then, from
           what I've heard!

BECKY   Well that's a surprise because Dr Bates next
           door is eighty-seven!

LEO   Behind closed doors though, eh?

           (*A beat.*)

BECKY   So is there anything else you need before I get
           off?

LEO   Couldn't make us another cuppa love, could
           you? This is like dish water!

BECKY   What do you fancy, Earl Grey or Blackcurrant
           Bracer?

LEO   I'm not bothered love. As long as it's hot and
           wet!

BECKY   Right.

(LEO *walks off past* BECKY *and exits. As he does this* RICH *enters, he is drying his hair with a towel and wears a dressing gown.*)

RICH   Bloody hell!

BECKY   There's some food in the freezer, but we're short of milk. And if they want a sandwich you can make them one with that ham, and there's a quiche in the fridge.

RICH   Just walked in on me in the shower!

BECKY   I'm going to be late if I don't get off.

RICH   Just walked in on me!

BECKY   What?

RICH   In the shower. I'm stood there bollock naked and he comes in and uses the loo. He's still sat there!

BECKY   Well they seem friendly enough.

RICH   That's a bit too bloody friendly!

BECKY   They've got to do what they've got to do!

RICH   How did they get in?

BECKY   I left a key under the mat.

                (RICH *looks around for any sign of the decorators.*)

RICH   Who are they?

BECKY   Eh?

RICH   Who are they?

BECKY   They're decorators!

RICH   I know that!

BECKY   They're the ones we could get at the price.

RICH	Ah, ah!
BECKY	Hardy and Hardy. They're local, I checked.
RICH	Hardy and Hardy?
BECKY	I think they're cousins.
RICH	Are you sure it's not Laurel and Hardy?
BECKY	They come in and do whatever, and then we never see them again!
RICH	Well, let's not get too "touchy feely"!
BECKY	What do you mean?
RICH	You'll be having a bloody whip-round for them before the week's out. I know you!
BECKY	Rich, they are only blokes!
RICH	I know they're only blokes.
BECKY	Well then?
RICH	I know all about blokes, I've been one for forty-five years!
BECKY	What are you saying?
RICH	They'll get where water won't.

(*A beat.*)

BECKY	What's wrong with them?
RICH	Well they share a brain for a start.
BECKY	I think they're cute.
RICH	Just comes and plonks himself down on the loo!
BECKY	They're all right!
RICH	Just watch 'em, that's all.

BECKY	You're going to be here, you watch 'em.
RICH	I will do!
	(BECKY *checks her watch.*)
BECKY	I'm going to have to go or I'll hit the traffic. Do you think you'll be all right?
RICH	I should be unless they keep walking in on me!
BECKY	What're you going to do?
RICH	I might help them, then we can get it done quicker! Cause if they're going be here for three weeks it'll drive me crackers!
BECKY	Six.
RICH	Eh?
BECKY	Six weeks!
	(LEO *enters with a roller, and a tray.*)
LEO	Oh aye, it'll be six weeks easy, a house this big.
RICH	I thought it was going to be three?
LEO	Never do this in three!
BECKY	Look give us a kiss . . . got to . . .
LEO	Don't mind me!
BECKY	I'll call you when I get there. Love you!
	(BECKY *and* RICH *kiss, it is a peck but deeply affectionate.* LEO *moves upstage but is aware.*)
RICH	And watch Grant . . .
BECKY	I haven't seen him in eight years.
RICH	He's a greaseball.

BECKY	Millionaire greaseball . . .
RICH	Exactly!
BECKY	I'll call you!
	(BECKY *departs.* RICH *watches her leave, he stands in silence.*)
LEO	A long drive!
RICH	Sorry?
LEO	Bath.
RICH	That's right.
LEO	Business and pleasure!
RICH	Yeh.
LEO	They say they never mix!
RICH	That's what they say.
	(DANNY *enters and looks concerned.*)
DANNY	You got a minute?
RICH	Why, what's wrong now?
DANNY	You've got a problem with the downstairs bog. I've tried to flush it but it's all backing up . . . Sorry about that, mate!
RICH	Oh right!
LEO	You couldn't see to it, could you?
DANNY	Yeh 'coz my stomach's a bit at the moment.
	(*A beat.*)
RICH	Oh, right!
LEO	Cheers, pal!

(LEO *switches the music back on. Music plays. Blackout.*)

Scene Four

10.15 am.

DANNY *is wiping down one of the walls, and generally fiddling around upstage.* LEO *is considering a number of large paint brushes.*

LEO	Has he un-blocked it yet?
DANNY	Dunno!
LEO	We needed it sorting though.
DANNY	I don't know what's happening to my arse at the moment!
LEO	Big bedrooms!
DANNY	All en-suite, aren't they?
	(*They work for a moment.*)
LEO	What do you reckon then?
DANNY	To what?
LEO	Becky!
DANNY	Oh, not really my . .
LEO	Nice though . . .
DANNY	Oh ar, nice but . . .
LEO	How do you score her?
DANNY	Low.
LEO	What?
DANNY	Low.

LEO	Give up . . .
DANNY	Well down!
LEO	You're dreaming.
DANNY	No, I've got her quite low!
LEO	I've got her down as half a shandy and bag of pork scratchings.
DANNY	What?
LEO	Oh, easy!
DANNY	No way . . .
LEO	Easily!
DANNY	She's nearly fifty.
LEO	You need some glasses . . .
DANNY	She looks fifty! And I'm doing her a favour!
LEO	Give up . . .
DANNY	Well please yourself, but she's four pints and a chicken korma for me!
LEO	No, mate!
DANNY	And a couple of chasers . . .
LEO	Your scoring system's all to cock.
DANNY	Yours is!
LEO	How is it?
DANNY	Well you scored that Sophia Lauren two whiskeys, and a Big Mac, and she's a bloody grandma!
LEO	You've no fucking taste, mate!

(RICH *enters. He is now dressed in smart casual clothes. He has just returned from sorting out the manhole.*)

RICH   That's all done . . .

LEO   You sorted it?

RICH   How are we doing in here?

LEO   Well another cup of tea wouldn't go amiss.

DANNY   Four sugars in mine, no milk.

RICH   We have no milk.

LEO   Well can't you get some?

RICH   We have none –

LEO   Isn't there a shop?

RICH   Yes!

DANNY   Send Sophie for some!

LEO   Aye, can't she get dressed and pop out for some?

DANNY   It'll not take her two minutes if she runs.

LEO   If she's going I'll have a Kit Kat! Does tha want owt, Dan?

DANNY   Aye she can get us a Mars bar, I'll give her t' money!

LEO   Aye go on, your lass said you'd look after us, didn't she?

RICH   I bet she did!

LEO   Oh aye, she said that you'd take care of us.

RICH   Did she?

            (*A beat.*)

DANNY	Don't like being on your own, then?
RICH	Sorry?
DANNY	She said you didn't like being on your own.
RICH	Well . . .
DANNY	Well you're all right now we're here, aren't you?
RICH	(*dead*) That's right.
DANNY	Aye, she gave us the full run down, didn't she?
LEO	Oh aye.
DANNY	Says you've got a lot of valuable stuff. Mind you, I told her not to worry – we'll make short work of that.
	(*All the men laugh. There is a sense of not knowing where the dividing line between joke and reality lies.*)
LEO	So you don't like Northern, then?
RICH	Sorry?
LEO	Northern Soul!
RICH	I don't know if I've ever heard any.
LEO	What, are you a Beatles fan?
RICH	No, not really. Jethro Tull, and The Who, Roger Whittaker . . .
LEO	Tha never got to Wigan Casino, then?
RICH	Not me.
LEO	Don't know what you're missing!
DANNY	Brilliant Wigan, wasn't it?
LEO	(*easily*) Tha never went!

DANNY	I was gunna go.
LEO	I went for a year on the trot! I paid a hundred quid for a single once, can you believe it? Good music; makes me feel twenty years younger.
RICH	No, I don't fancy that!
LEO	You're the only bloke I've met who doesn't!
RICH	Twenty years ago I was wondering what life was all about!
LEO	And now you know?
RICH	Well . . . ?
LEO	There you go then?
RICH	No, I wouldn't want to go back . . .
LEO	Sounds sad, mate.
RICH	No, my knees are bad, so dancing's had it. You should see me in a morning . . .
DANNY	We saw you!
LEO	They have these Northern nights . . . brilliant, aren't they?
RICH	What, were you a mod?
LEO	Part skin, part mod.
RICH	A skod, then?
LEO	Mind you we're all in our forties now, like . . . so there's not a lot of trouble but we still like to party.
RICH	Very nice.

DANNY	I bet it's all party party at them college re-unions and all, isn't it? I mean I wouldn't let our lass go off by herself . . .
LEO	You should see their lass!
RICH	Yeh?
LEO	She's all rate.
DANNY	Mind you, they're all sophisticated aren't they?
RICH	Who?
DANNY	That university lot.
RICH	Well, I don't know about that . . .
DANNY	Oh aye, they don't let it get to 'em; they're shagging each other's brains out but it's nowt to 'em, is it?
RICH	Do you think so?
DANNY	Oh aye man, they don't think twice about it!
LEO	That's rate, I mean look at that one who was having an affair wi't mother and then wi't daughter, dirty bastard!
DANNY	They put 'em in jail on our estate for that.
LEO	Be rate Dan, everybody's doing that on your estate.
DANNY	Then he goes and writes his memoirs about it and makes a bloody fortune.
LEO	I think I might do that. Confessions of a painter and decorator! Does tha think it'd sell?
DANNY	Well I wouldn't fuckin' buy it!
LEO	Why not?

DANNY	I'd write my own.
LEO	Tha can't write, can tha?
DANNY	Tha can't paint but tha makes a fuckin' living out of it!

(DANNY *and* LEO *laugh loudly*.)

RICH	Can we just keep the language down?
LEO	What?
RICH	Do you mind keeping the language . . .
DANNY	Aye, sorry mate, just slips out.
RICH	I mean I'm not a prude, but –
DANNY	Tha'll not want to come out with us then! We go fuckin' crackers!
LEO	What's he just said, you thick twat!
DANNY	Sorry.
RICH	Hey listen . . . I've been there . . . done that, got the T-shirt!
DANNY	Oh. Oh! Have you heard him . . .
RICH	No, listen . . .
LEO	A couple of Red Bulls and tha'll be laughing.

(RICH *is feeling uncomfortable*.)

RICH	Becky said it was going to take six weeks.
LEO	Could be longer.
RICH	No chance of getting some other men on?
LEO	No we take our time, I mean I admit we're not the fastest, but if you want some cowboys you can get somebody else, we make a job of it.
RICH	Right.

DANNY   Oh aye, you'll get to know us by the time we finish.

RICH   That'll be good then!

             (LEO *crosses to the CD player.*)

LEO   Here hang on, let's see if he likes this . . .

RICH   What?

LEO   Listen to some of this, see if you like it?

RICH   No, I'd better let you get on.

LEO   Hang on, just have a listen . . .

RICH   No, I'd better let you get on or it might take you eight weeks!

LEO   Well ar, that's true!

RICH   I'll go and get some milk!

LEO   And a Kit Kat!

DANNY   Mars bar for me!

RICH   One Kit Kat and a pint of milk.

LEO   Have you got some money?

RICH   Yes, yes, don't worry about that. I'll see to it. Shall I get some crumpets and bread rolls for anybody?

LEO   Aye, go on then, I like a bit of crumpet.

RICH   Yes, yes . . . very good!

             (RICH *exits.* LEO *and* DANNY *watch him go.*)

DANNY   Nice bloke.

LEO   Mmmm . . .

DANNY   Bit of a wanker.

LEO   Arsehole! Turn t' music up.

                       (DANNY *turns the music up as they resume*
                       their work. Music. Blackout.)

                       Scene Five

4.00 pm.

DANNY *and* LEO *are packing away some of their kit. Ladders*
are being struck, and planks taken down. DANNY *is reading*
the Daily Sport. LEO *is content to wipe down a number of*
brushes.

LEO   Time is it ?

DANNY   Nearly four . . .

LEO   That'll do for today . . .

DANNY   Shall I start packing . . . ?

LEO   Is your lass gunna be . . .

DANNY   I think so . . .

LEO   We'll meet in t' Admiral . . .

DANNY   Is Val . . . ?

LEO   Oh aye, no trouble, looking forward to it she
                       says.

DANNY   That's all rate then!

LEO   Leave them dust sheets, it'll save us a job
                       tomorrow.

                       (RICH *enters from upstage. He is on a cordless*
                       phone speaking to BECKY.)

RICH   I was beginning to wonder. You got there OK,
                       then? No, you're breaking up. As long as

you're all right, that's fine . . . Are you going
to call me later? . . . 'Love you'.

(RICH *sheepishly puts the phone down in the
room.*)

LEO	She got there, then?
RICH	Bad traffic . . . five hours.
LEO	Getting a bit worried?
RICH	Well, you never know, do you?
LEO	I thought . . . I told him!
RICH	Well, she's there now, anyway!
LEO	That's good, then.
RICH	She has an old friend from college who has just hit the jackpot with one of these Dot Com companies. He was always a jet-setter by all accounts . . . so. . .
LEO	She'll be sniffing around him, then?
RICH	Well . . .
LEO	We're all like dogs, sniffing about, aren't we?
RICH	Well . . .
LEO	That's how it all works though, isn't it? Rotary meetings, business lunches, after-dinner speeches. They call it networking now, we used to call it arse-licking. Mind you, that's how we work, isn't it?
DANNY	(*still packing away*) Oh aye, my calendar's that full of after-dinner speeches I haven't got time for a shit!
LEO	Mind you, she'll not get up to owt daft, will she?
RICH	How do you mean?

LEO	She doesn't strike me as the type who'd do owt stupid?
RICH	Well I don't . . .
DANNY	Friendly though.
LEO	Oh aye, friendly . . .
RICH	Well yes . . .
LEO	But she's not a prick teaser, is she?
RICH	Hey?
DANNY	Some of 'em are.
RICH	Are they?
LEO	You'd be surprised.
RICH	Do you reckon?
LEO	Ugh . . . some of 'em.
RICH	Ah well . . .
	(LEO *and* DANNY *continue to pack up*.)
LEO	So what have you got planned for tonight?
RICH	Get a take-away and watch a video. I might even do some ironing . . . I like to, erm . . .
LEO	Bloody hell, you're easily pleased!
RICH	Thought I'd just take it easy.
LEO	I can't stop in when I've been inside all day. Especially on a weekend!
RICH	Well you know . . . it comes to us all!
LEO	You're living the wrong life.
RICH	No, I'm not –
DANNY	I am –

(LEO *finishes packing and is about ready to depart.*)

LEO   Right, that's us just about done. Anyway, we'll see you tomorra, early. We've got a key.

RICH   I'd better give you the code.

LEO   1848. We've got that, so if you're in bed . . .

(SOPHIE *enters. She is dressed for a concert. LEO and DANNY are about to depart. They take a number of ladders and paint cans with them.*)

DANNY   Here she is, look!

LEO   Aye, and she's got dressed and all, look!

DANNY   Didn't recognise her with her clothes on did you?

LEO   Anyway, we're going . . .

DANNY   Yeh, I want to get myself a pint of milk.

LEO   And I fancy a Guinness . . . See you!

(LEO *and* DANNY *exit.* SOPHIE *makes a face as they leave. Silence.*)

RICH   What?

SOPHIE   Goorr . . .

RICH   Yeah . . . well?

SOPHIE   Bloody idiots!

RICH   Now, don't be a snob . . .

SOPHIE   I'm not.

RICH   A bit scary, but –

SOPHIE   Do they scare you?

RICH   How the other half live!

SOPHIE	I thought all that had stopped.
RICH	Ah . . . what?
SOPHIE	All the innuendos!
RICH	I had mates like that.
SOPHIE	Oh, come on?
RICH	Well maybe not quite like that.
SOPHIE	Basic mammals!
RICH	Hey!
SOPHIE	Well they are.
RICH	There but for the grace of God . . . !
SOPHIE	You're joking?
RICH	No . . . I'm not.
	(SOPHIE *checks her tickets and car keys*.)
SOPHIE	Right. Tickets . . . car keys!
RICH	Where are you going, anyway?
SOPHIE	Manchester! Shed Seven are on.
RICH	What are they a band or a warehouse?
SOPHIE	Ha ha!
RICH	Watch what you're doing.
SOPHIE	Don't turn into an old fart, Dad!
RICH	It's too late!
SOPHIE	It's a crazy world out there, you know . . .
RICH	It is . . .
SOPHIE	You've just got to find it!

RICH   You don't see it like I do!

SOPHIE   I know, but you keep bloody telling me! See
                you, love you . . . Will you be all right?

RICH   Why, what do you think I'm going to do?

SOPHIE   See you!

                (SOPHIE *exits.* RICH *stands on his own, and
                surveys the work that* LEO *and* DANNY *have
                been doing. He looks at the walls and the dust
                sheets that have been left on the floor. He
                looks at the mess. He then picks up the mobile
                phone.*)

RICH   Is that Fung Wah? Is that Fung Wah? I'd like
                to order a take-away. A take-away? You're not
                doing take-aways? . . . Why not? Because of
                the petrol shortage! What petrol
                shortage? I thought that was all sorted? . . .
                You've heard a rumour it's going to start
                again! But it's just a rumour . . . No, I said . . .
                It's just a rumour it's not a fact . . . OK! No, I'm
                not being funny! Not at all, I was just . . . All I
                want to do is eat . . . OK? So do you have a
                table for one? For one! Ron who? No, not Ron,
                one, a table for one . . . You'll have a look . . .
                You do, half what? Half eight? Right, thank
                you, I'll be there!

                (RICH *ends his call.*)

                That's that, then!

                (RICH *exits. Music. Blackout.*)

                              Scene Six

The City. 8.30 pm.

*The scene changes as all the dust sheets are struck by the
actors playing* LEO, DANNY, *and* VAL. *They are all dressed in
decorators overalls, and make short work of clearing the*

'House' setting. This reveals a huge blue box which represents the city and the night time. All this is done as a dance. Into the middle of this comparatively huge operatic space is revealed a table. RICH *sits at the table as the* FIRST WAITER, *(the actress playing* SOPHIE) *enters. She offers* RICH *a large menu.*

RICH	(*taking the menu*) Thank you!
1ST WAITER	You ready?
RICH	Well I've only just got the . . .
1ST WAITER	You ready order?
RICH	I've only just . . .
1ST WAITER	You want drink?
RICH	Diet Coke . . .
1ST WAITER	Glass?
RICH	Bottle . . .
1ST WAITER	You want chop stick?
RICH	No, I'm all thumbs . . .
1ST WAITER	You ready order?
RICH	Erm . . . Set meal for one please!
1ST WAITER	Set meawl . . . A or B or C?
RICH	Oh, can I phone a friend?
1ST WAITER	You want pay phone?
RICH	No, I'll have B, eh? Let's be adventurous!
1ST WAITER	Set meawl B . . . Thank you . . .
	(*As* 1ST WAITER *exits, the* 2ND WAITER (*played by the actor playing* DANNY) *enters and approaches* RICH'S *table.*)
2ND WAITER	You ready order?

RICH   I've just ordered.

2ND WAITER   You ready order?

RICH   I've just ordered.

2ND WAITER   You want drink?

RICH   I've just ordered.

2ND WAITER   You want chop stick or knife an for?

RICH   Knife and for. . .

2ND WAITER   I have good bottoe wed wine!

RICH   I've just ordered, thanks.

2ND WAITER   You order glass?

RICH   Bottle.

2ND WAITER   I bring bottoe?

RICH   A bottle of Coke.

2ND WAITER   One bottoe Coke de Rhone!

                        (*As* 2ND WAITER *exits*, 1ST WAITER *re-enters with
                        a bowl of soup.*)

1ST WAITER   Chicken mushroom?

RICH   If that's what it said.

1ST WAITER   Set meawl for Ron B?

RICH   Thats me, Ron B!

1ST WAITER   Enjoy your meawl.

RICH   Any chance of getting a spoon?

                        (1ST WAITER *exits, as* 2ND WAITER *returns with a
                        bottle of red wine.*)

2ND WAITER   Wed wine?

RICH	Erm . . .
2ND WAITER	Bottoe wed wine?
RICH	Oh, go on then!
2ND WAITER	You try?
RICH	No, thank you.
2ND WAITER	You try?
RICH	Yes, of course . . .

(2ND WAITER *pours the wine, as* 1ST WAITER *brings a spoon for* RICH. *He sips the wine.*)

2ND WAITER	You like?
RICH	Lovely . . .

(RICH *sips at the wine, and the* 2ND WAITER *fills his glass once more.*)

2ND WAITER	Enjoy your meawl . . .
RICH	I'll try . . .

(*Both* WAITERS *exit, as* RICH *begins to tuck into his meal. As he does,* LEO, *dressed for a night on the town, enters the Chinese restaurant, and approaches* RICH'S *table. There is embarrassing tension.*)

LEO	Now then?
RICH	Arh!

(*A beat.*)

LEO	How you doing?
RICH	Good, thanks!
LEO	Well, well!
RICH	That's right . . .

(*A beat.*)

LEO   Decided to . . .

RICH   Yes!

LEO   Oh . . . right.

RICH   Yes, a bit of the old . . .

(*A beat.*)

LEO   Sophie get there?

RICH   Yes!

LEO   Good.

RICH   You know, growing up . . . bands . . .
           boyfriends . . .

(*A beat.*)

LEO   I couldn't believe it when I saw you . . .

RICH   Well there you go . . .

(*A beat.*)

LEO   I thought you said you were staying . . .

RICH   You on your own, or . . . ?

LEO   No, I'm . . . with the wife.

RICH   Oh right, well . . .

LEO   She's just nipped for a . . . (*A beat.*) I'll join
           you, shall I?

RICH   Eh?

LEO   I'll just have five minutes . . .

RICH   Do you think she'll . . .?

(LEO *makes himself comfortable at* RICH'S
table.)

LEO   So how's it looking?

RICH   The food?

LEO   The stuff we've put on? Drying all right, is it?
It's a bastard sometimes, if it doesn't dry right,
it's a nightmare sanding it. And that emulsion?

RICH   Yes?

LEO   I didn't like to tell Becky when she ordered it
but it's notorious for streaking.

RICH   Is it?

LEO   Oh, bloody hell!

RICH   Oh, well . . .

LEO   So has she rang, then?

RICH   Well . . . no . . .

(LEO *bursts into laughter.*)

LEO   Arggh!

RICH   What?

LEO   Oh, man . . .

RICH   What?

LEO   There you go . . .

RICH   What?

LEO   Must be having a good time?

RICH   Well I suppose . . .

LEO   Letting her hair down . . .

RICH   Quite possibly . . .

LEO   Maybe we were wrong about her.

RICH   How do you mean?

LEO   (*noticing* VAL) Oh, oh, the boss is here, look!

             (VAL *enters. She is a strikingly attractive
             woman in her early forties. Vulgar and
             aggressive, she is also dripping with fake
             gold; and has an unstoppable cleavage –
             which would turn any head.*)

VAL   I wondered where you'd bloody got to!

LEO   I say, look who's here!

VAL   Who is it?

LEO   It's Richard whatsit.

VAL   Oh, right!

LEO   This is Val!

RICH   Hello.

VAL   Hello darlin'.

RICH   Hello!

LEO   We're doing his . . .

VAL   Are they making a job of it?

RICH   Well we've got the wrong paint, but –

VAL   You tell me if they're not –

LEO   Val's the boss.

             (VAL *stands, wondering if they are staying.*)

VAL   Are we sitting . . . ?

LEO   Course we are, I . . .

             (VAL *sits at the table and lights a cigarette.*
             LEO *plays with the menu.*)

VAL	Don't mind if I smoke, do you love?
RICH	(*he does*) No, not if you . . .
VAL	He hates it, but –
LEO	She does what she wants.
VAL	He can't tell me what to do, can he?
LEO	Not all the time.
VAL	None of the bloody time!
LEO	I can't bloody control her, to be honest.
VAL	I don't want controlling!
LEO	What've you got there, then?
RICH	Chicken and mushroom soup, without the chicken, I think!
VAL	I hate Chinese, it makes me gip!
RICH	You'll like this.
VAL	Will I?
RICH	I dont think its ever seen China!
LEO	Their lass has cleared off and gone to Bath for the weekend!
RICH	Oh it's er . . .
LEO	Hob-nobbing with millionaires!
VAL	Lucky for some!
RICH	Well . . .
VAL	She's hobnobbing with millionaires and he's sat here with us!
LEO	I wonder who's having the best time?

VAL	I could guess!
RICH	(*to himself*) Yes, so could I!
	(*A beat.*)
LEO	She's gone to a college thing.
VAL	She says . . .
RICH	No, they have these reunions every eight years. They have them at the place I went to but I don't . . .
VAL	No?
RICH	I don't think I could face it.
VAL	Too many skeletons?
RICH	Some!
VAL	Oh hell!
	(*Silence.* VAL *smokes.*)
LEO	He's a painter, in't tha?
VAL	A what?
LEO	He's an artist.
VAL	You should live in our house.
LEO	He's got a picture in't post office, an't tha?
VAL	You'd paint some bloody pictures then! And they'd be all nudes.
RICH	Really?
VAL	He's never get his bloody clothes on!
RICH	Oh dear!
VAL	Always hanging out, he is!
RICH	Oh, right!

VAL	Aye they'd all he bloody dodgy pictures if he lived with you.
LEO	Maybe they are!
RICH	Well, some of them are surreal.
VAL	They'd be chuffin' surreal if you lived with him!
RICH	I bet they would!
	(*A beat.*)
LEO	Val did some modelling you know, didn't you?
VAL	Oh don't . . .
LEO	She did!
VAL	Years ago . . .
RICH	Did you?
VAL	Years ago.
LEO	Good, though.
VAL	Just for a magazine, wasn't it?
LEO	Topless stuff.
RICH	Oh!
LEO	Brilliant man, you should see 'em.
RICH	Well . . .
VAL	Tasteful, weren't they?
LEO	I'll bring some to show you, shall I?
VAL	He doesn't want to be looking at me wi' nowt on, you soft git! Do you . . . ?
RICH	Well . . .

VAL	You don't know how to answer that, do you?
RICH	Well . . .
VAL	I say, he don't know how to answer that!
	(LEO *and* VAL *find* RICH'S *embarrassment amusing.*)
LEO	Hey if you ever want a model . . . ?
RICH	That's right!
VAL	You never know?
	(LEO *is looking at the wine list.*)
LEO	What do you fancy then, kid?
VAL	I'll just have a spritzer.
LEO	I'm gagging. Are you in for one Rich?
RICH	No, I'm all right actually. I didn't want this, I ordered a coke.
VAL	I'm bloody gagging, I am!
LEO	I say, I tried to get him to listen to some Northern this morning but he wasn't interested.
RICH	Well, it was half past seven.
VAL	Don't you like it?
LEO	He's not heard any . . . Roger Whittaker, he says.
RICH	I was joking . . . I don't mind soul music as such, but . . .
VAL	We love it don't we? We go all over! Leeds, Grimsby! It's coming back, you know?
RICH	Is it really?
VAL	There's a good night in Bury, isn't there?

LEO	Aye that's not bad!
VAL	And there's a good night in Stoke. There's a weekender coming up in Cleethorpes! Blackpool Mecca wa' brilliant!
LEO	You'll have to come wi' us. Bring your lass.
VAL	Is she into it?
RICH	I wouldn't have thought . . .
VAL	I bet we've got two thousand records . . . What do you reckon, Leo?
	(LEO *rises from the table.*)
LEO	I'm just going to nip for a squirt . . . shalln't be a minute. You have a chat to Val . . . keep her busy.
VAL	What's he like . . . ?
RICH	Ha!
	(LEO *makes his excuses to leave.* VAL *gets comfy with* RICH. *Silence.* RICH *can't help but keep glancing at her bust.*)
VAL	Nice in here!
RICH	I haven't been for a couple of . . .
	(*Silence.*)
VAL	(*innocent*) He says it's nice and big.
RICH	Sorry?
VAL	The house! I'll have to come and have a look!
RICH	Well it's not a mansion . . .
VAL	Well he seems taken with it.
RICH	Oh, right . . .

VAL	He says he's going to enjoy doing it . . .
RICH	We've only been in it two months. It's all got to be done, a bit of a tip at the moment.
VAL	They can't do any damage, then?
RICH	Why, do they usually?
VAL	No, just the odd party!
RICH	Yes, well, it's perfect for parties. You can't breath for dust sheets left all over!
VAL	Oh, no parties.
RICH	Don't you like them?
VAL	Oh no, I love a good session.
RICH	Oh . . . right then.
VAL	But I usually drink too much . . .
RICH	Oh dear.
VAL	Oh, I like a drink.
RICH	Well, I used to but . . .
VAL	Always have . . .
RICH	I don't have as much now . . . but erm . . .
VAL	And when I've had a few . . .
RICH	Yeh?
VAL	Oh!
RICH	Oh dear . . .
VAL	Mind you, it's like I've said to him, I'm forty-three, I can't embarrass myself much more.
RICH	You've done all there is to do, have you?

VAL	Twice over, love . . . I've done it all!
RICH	Oh dear!
VAL	I've said to him, nowt shocks me any more!
RICH	Well there you go . . .
VAL	No, it's true, that . . . nowt shocks me.
RICH	I know what you mean!
VAL	You read about stuff in the papers, kids getting um . . .
RICH	I know . . .
VAL	Bloody affairs!
RICH	I know.
VAL	This, that and the other . . . he's run off with her . . .
RICH	That's right . . .
VAL	She's forty, he's thirteen . . . I mean, thirteen?
RICH	Absolutely.
VAL	What's he doing for her at thirteen?
RICH	I've no idea!
VAL	Or he's eighty and she's –
RICH	That's right.
VAL	I mean . . .
RICH	I know . . .
VAL	And that mother who killed her own –
RICH	I know.
VAL	I've said to him, human beings . . .

RICH   I know . . .

VAL   Bloody pathetic, love . . .

RICH   I know.

VAL   No . . . nowt shocks me.

RICH   No!

VAL   Nowt surprises me any more!

RICH   No, I know what you mean.

VAL   I wish she'd come for some bastard drinks, I'm
         gagging!

         (LEO *returns, and sits.*)

LEO   That's better.

VAL   Are we going to get a drink . . . ?

LEO   She says she's coming.

RICH   Listen, I'd better let you get on . . .

         (RICH *shuffles and wipes his mouth with a
         napkin.*)

LEO   Are you going?

RICH   I am, to be honest . . .

VAL   Aren't you having the rest?

RICH   To be honest . . . it's not . . .

VAL   Aren't you so well?

RICH   No, it's just . . . I'm not really so hungry, you
         know. And I can't drink all this, so . . .

VAL   Well, we'll have that!

RICH	Be my guest. I'll just get the bill . . . I might do a bit of work in the studio, to be honest. Sorry to . . . (*To* VAL.) Nice to meet you . . .

(RICH *is almost standing.*)

VAL	Lovely to meet you, it's nice to see the people he works with.

(VAL *stands and pecks* RICH. *It is rather sensitive and a little too familiar. She returns to her seat.*)

Take it steady out there, it's bedlam on a Friday!

RICH	It is, isn't it?
LEO	I'll see you tomorrow.
RICH	Have a good night!
LEO	I will do, and I hope Becky doesn't get too drunk.
RICH	Oh don't worry about that!
LEO	I don't want to be working in a house where there's a bad atmosphere.
RICH	No, right! Thanks a lot. Good night.
VAL	Night.
LEO	Night.

(RICH *exits.* VAL *and* LEO *consider the menu.*)

VAL	Nice bloke!
LEO	Oh ar!
VAL	So what are you having then?
LEO	(*head in the menu*) I don't know what I fancy.
VAL	I might have his . . .

LEO	It's a thought!
VAL	Do you want a glass of this?
LEO	Aye, I can do!
VAL	Waste not, want not!

(VAL *pours* LEO *a glass of wine.* VAL *and* LEO *laugh.*)

LEO	Mmm nice . . .
VAL	Good taste, anyway . . .
LEO	Right, I'll have a set meal for two! What do you want?

(*Music. Blackout.*)

Scene Seven

City. 9.15 pm.

The Chinese restaurant table is cleared, as a kind of dance, by the actress playing SOPHIE, *who is dressed as a waiter.* DANNY *dances with a street light from upstage.* RICH *enters. He gets his car keys from his pocket, and takes out a mobile. He dials in* BECKY'S *number.* RICH *moves around as he speaks.*

RICH   (*on the mobile*) It's me . . . How's it going? Can
                 you talk? . . . I must have forgot to put the
                 answer machine on . . . Fung Wah's, they
                 reckon the petrol's . . . Who are you with?
                 Grant's there, is he . . . How's it going? Listen
                 I'm losing you . . . Have a good . . . (*To
                 himself.*) Bloody hell!

                 (*He has lost the signal, and gets out his car
                 keys. As he does* DANNY *enters, dressed up for
                 the night.*)

DANNY   Now then?

RICH	How you doing?
DANNY	Getting pissed . . .
RICH	Ah, great!
DANNY	Where are you going?
RICH	Home!
DANNY	I thought you said you could take it?
RICH	What?
DANNY	Got the T-shirt, you said!
RICH	Yes, but it doesn't fit me.
DANNY	Hey, do you want to meet our lass – Vicky?
RICH	Listen, if she's busy . . .
DANNY	No she's . . . (*Shouts off.*) Come here, you soft bitch! She can't hear me . . . Vicky? She can't hear me. Look at her having a pee in the street, the soft cow . . . Would you credit it?
RICH	Anyway, have a good night . . .
DANNY	All right, have a good night . . . (*Shouts.*) Vicky . . . Hang on, you soft pig!
	(RICH *watches as they go.* CARRIE *enters like a dance. She is a young prostitute who looks much the worse for drugs and drink. She spots* RICH *and waves at him . . .* CARRIE *makes her way downstage towards* RICH.)
CARRIE	Got a light, love?
RICH	Sorry?
CARRIE	A light?
RICH	No, sorry.

CARRIE	You looking for business?
RICH	Eh?
CARRIE	Business . . .
RICH	Me? No thanks love . . . I've already got one your age.
CARRIE	Come on darling . . .
RICH	Not for me.
CARRIE	I'll give you a hand job . . .
RICH	I'm not bothered, thanks.
CARRIE	Ten quid.
RICH	No thanks.
CARRIE	We can go down Myton street for a quickie if you want? I'll use my mouth.
RICH	No I think I'll leave it, thanks.
CARRIE	Twenty quid and I'll do a full strip in your car.

(RICH *reaches into his pocket and gives* CARRIE *a twenty pound note.*)

RICH	I tell you what . . . Here you are, look.
CARRIE	Oh, right. What do you want?
RICH	Nothing.
CARRIE	What?
RICH	I don't want anything. There's twenty quid, call it a good deal. Just leave me alone, I'm not interested, all right?
CARRIE	Why not?
RICH	'Coz I don't.
CARRIE	Don't you fancy me?

RICH	Eh?
CARRIE	Don't you fancy me . . . ?
RICH	Well . . .
CARRIE	What?
RICH	Not really . . .
CARRIE	Oh, right.
RICH	Sorry.
CARRIE	Well that's nice, innit?
RICH	Look you've got twenty quid, now bugger off!
CARRIE	Well that's fuckin' charmin', innit?
RICH	What?
CARRIE	That's really rich that is.
RICH	Hey look . . .

(CARRIE *peels away from* RICH *and begins
yelling at him.*)

CARRIE	Freak . . .
RICH	Eh?
CARRIE	Bastard!
RICH	What?
CARRIE	Bastard!
RICH	Wow, hang on!
CARRIE	Weirdo!
RICH	Hey listen –
CARRIE	Freak –

RICH	What?
CARRIE	You bloody freak!

(CARRIE *starts to walk away from* RICH.)

RICH	Well give us my twenty quid back then, you sad cow!

(*As she exits upstage,* LEO *enters from the opposite upstage entrance.* CARRIE *has gone.*)

LEO	Arggghhh!
RICH	Eh?
LEO	What have you been up to . . . ?
RICH	I was just . . .
LEO	Argghh!
RICH	What?
LEO	Dirty sod!
RICH	Hey listen . . .
LEO	Arrrgh . . .
RICH	No, I was just going . . .
LEO	What's your lass going to say about that?
RICH	Hey –

(LEO *turns and shouts, off.*)

LEO	Val! Look who's here!

(VAL *enters, slightly looser than of previous.*)

VAL	I thought you were going home?
RICH	I was, but –
LEO	Right, are we in the Admiral, then?

RICH	No, I'm going, to have to –
VAL	You said that last time!
LEO	He's trying to avoid us.
RICH	Not at all, I was just going to my car, and she came up to me, can't have been eighteen!
VAL	Said he was going to do some work!
LEO	Now we know what sort!
RICH	No, honestly!
LEO	You can come for a drink with us you know, can't he?
VAL	Course he can!
RICH	It's nice of you but . . .
LEO	We're meeting our Dan and Vicky!
VAL	You'll love Vicky, she's a right laugh!
RICH	Aye, I've just seen her actually.
VAL	Come on, what's up with you?
RICH	Well it's not fair to spoil your night . . .
VAL	Oh, don't be daft!
RICH	No, honestly.
LEO	Bollocks!
RICH	Sorry?
LEO	Bollocks!
RICH	Hey, look . . .
LEO	(angry, loud) I said, bollocks, tha's coming for a drink!
RICH	No, honest, listen!

LEO   Bollocks, tha's coming! Tha's coming for a
               drink, I'm buying thee a drink. Now is tha
               gunna accept it, or are we gunna fall out about
               it?

               (*Silence.*)

RICH   I'll have one . . .

               (*Lights. Music.*)

                        Scene Eight

The Admiral. 9.30 pm.

DANNY *and* VICKY *enter. They have attached to them life-sized
puppets.* LEO, VAL *and* RICH *all crush together to give the
impression that they are in an extremely crowded pub. Silly
String is sprayed from the characters upstage of the main trio.
All have drinks with them. They are lit very tightly and the
atmosphere is heavy with smoke. Everyone has to shout above
the noise.*

LEO   Now then! Look who we've got!

DANNY   How, are you doing?

RICH   Oh, you know . . .

LEO   We caught him loitering.

VAL   With intent!

DANNY   I thought you were going home?

RICH   I was.

DANNY   Good fuckin' laugh in here. Sorry, mate – this is
               Vicky.

RICH   I saw her earlier.

VICKY   You what?

DANNY   We're doing his house up.

VAL	Brilliant, in't it?
RICH	What?
VAL	Brilliant in here.
RICH	I can't hear myself think.
VAL	What?
RICH	I can't . . . forget it.
LEO	Good atmosphere in here!
RICH	Absolutely!
LEO	Do you want another?
RICH	I'm only having . . .
LEO	So did you see the match, then?
RICH	No, I don't really –
LEO	England what a mess, what's happening to English football?
RICH	I've no idea.
LEO	We've got a Swede now and all.
RICH	So I understand.
LEO	I mean we had a fuckin' turnip and now we've got a swede!
RICH	I don't really follow.
DANNY	Fuckin' England are shit. Sorry, Rich.
RICH	No problem.
LEO	They are.
DANNY	England are shite, aren't they?
RICH	That's right.

DANNY	We invent the game and we're shite! Sorry mate, I –
VICKY	You what?
DANNY	England!
VICKY	Shit aren't they?
RICH	They should bring Alf Ramsey back.
DANNY	It'd be a bloody miracle if they did!
LEO	Not much of a football fan?
RICH	I think they pay them too much.
DANNY	Who do you support, then?
RICH	Nobody.
DANNY	Everybody supports somebody.
RICH	Not me. I think they should shoot 'em all!
DANNY	He's got a point!
VICKY	You what?
	(VAL *struggles to get near* RICH.)
VAL	When did you last come around town, then?
RICH	Now you're asking?
LEO	(*to* RICH) You coming round the Old Town?
VAL	Course he is.
RICH	Hey, hang on . . .
LEO	You'll be all rate wi' us . . . Nobody'll touch you.
RICH	Oh, it's not that . . .
LEO	There shouldn't be any trouble anyway.

RICH	Hey, don't worry about that.
LEO	Can handle yourself, can you?
RICH	No, I'm not –
LEO	Bit of a tough nut, eh?
RICH	Well . . .
LEO	You need to be when you're out!
RICH	I'm all right.
LEO	Danny reckons he's a hard case.
DANNY	We should be all rate, then!
RICH	Hey, listen . . .
DANNY	Any trouble and we'll leave it to you, shall we?
RICH	No, I'm not saying that –
VAL	Hey, we don't want any bloody fighting tonight. I'm fed up of it!
VICKY	(*to* VAL) You what?
LEO	He'll be all rate with us!
DANNY	It's good down the Old Town . . .
RICH	I dunno if I'm –
	(LEO *fights his way back to* VICKY.)
LEO	All right then, Vicky?
VICKY	You what?
LEO	Looks like being a good night.
VICKY	You what?
LEO	You looking forward to it?
VICKY	You what?

LEO	You'll be all right.
VICKY	Should be a good night.
LEO	You what?
VICKY	I've only had three!
LEO	You what?
VICKY	Can't wait to get down there!
DANNY	(*to* LEO) Is he coming down?
LEO	Course he is!
RICH	(*shouting to* LEO) Hey, listen!
LEO	Take no notice!
DANNY	(*to* RICH) It's a good night!
	(VAL *is being pushed towards* RICH.)
VAL	This is cosy!
RICH	What?
VAL	You could get to know somebody very well in here.
	(LEO *fights his way back to* VAL.)
LEO	All right?
RICH	Yeh, yeh!
VAL	I say, its a good job he's not a prude.
LEO	Where did you say Sophie had gone?
RICH	Manchester.
LEO	Becky said she'll be out of her head this weekend!
RICH	Well . . .

LEO	I like to get out of my head at the weekend!
VAL	He's like a big kid at heart!
LEO	I like to let my hair down.
RICH	It's bloody crackers in here!
LEO	Don't you like it?
RICH	Well . . .
LEO	It's all right, isn't it?
RICH	Well yeh, but –
LEO	We can go if you want?
RICH	No, no.
LEO	We'll go somewhere if you want!
RICH	Hey, don't do it for me!
LEO	No, come on . . .
RICH	What?
LEO	We'll get off.
RICH	No, no.
LEO	(*to* DANNY) Danny, sup up!
RICH	Oh no, Leo, listen . . .
LEO	(*loudly*) Right, everybody sup up.
RICH	No honest Leo, really, don't mind me, mate!
LEO	Come on sup up, Rich doesn't like it in here. Let's get straight down the Old Town for a couple!
VAL	What?
LEO	We're off!
VICKY	You what?

LEO   Rich thinks it's shit in here!

RICH   Hey no, it's all right . . . honest!

VAL   There's no bloody room!

DANNY   It's full of twats in here!

VICKY   You what?

DANNY   Shut up, you!

RICH   Listen, don't let me . . .

VAL   Where're we going ?

LEO   We'll have a couple in the back room of the Old
               Town.

VICKY   You what?

LEO   (*to* RICH) You'll love it in there, man!

RICH   Yeh?

LEO   We'll be able to have a good natter in there!

VAL   It's a bit rough, though!

LEO   Listen . . . don't worry about it. Rich reckons
               he's a right hard case. We'll all be all right wi'
               him! Won't we?

RICH   That's right . . .

LEO   Right, come on – Sup up!

               (*Lights. Music.*)

Scene Nine

The Old Town. 10.30 pm.

*Music plays under. The Admiral setting revolves, to reveal
another pub interior. Only* VICKY, LEO, VAL *and* DANNY *are on
stage. The puppets are seen through translucent flatage.
Everyone has a replenished drink.*

LEO	(*over the music*) What do you . . .
RICH	Yeh, well . . .
LEO	(*loudly*) It's rough in here . . .
RICH	Well . . . ?
LEO	I had my nose broken as a kid!
RICH	Yeh?
LEO	Three times . . .
VAL	He's all tense, aren't you?
RICH	No, I'm fine . . .
VAL	Are you having another drink?
RICH	No . . . I'm going to get off after this.
LEO	Have another, man . . .
RICH	I'm driving . . .
LEO	Get a taxi . . . !
DANNY	(*to* VICKY) Do you want another, Vick?
VICKY	(*to* DANNY) You what?
VAL	Have another drink, man . . .
RICH	No I'm . . .
VAL	What's a matter with you . . . ?
RICH	Well when you get to a certain age . . .
LEO	Oh here we go . . .
RICH	Two glasses of wine and I'm singing.
DANNY	Get him on't karaoke!
RICH	It creeps up on you!

VAL   Oh, give up . . .

RICH   One minute I'm at art school, and the next thing
               you know I'm shouting at kids in the street.

VAL   That's sad!

RICH   Telling 'em to pick litter up . . .

LEO   Listen, life begins at forty . . .

RICH   I don't know who the hell said that but they
               were talking out of their back end!

VICKY   (*to* DANNY) I'm going to have to pop to t' bog.

DANNY   (*to* VICKY) You what?

VICKY   I'm bursting!

               (VICKY *makes to exit.*)

RICH   I thought it was something that happened to
               other people.

VAL   What?

RICH   Middle age.

VAL   (*drinking*) You're not middle aged!

RICH   You should see me in a morning.

VAL   Yeh?

RICH   It's all heading down hill!

VAL   Oh, don't . . .

RICH   (*shouting*) Listen, I've got a physique like a
               little lad's willy!

LEO   We can see that!

VAL   He's still toned, aren't you?

RICH   I had a physique once, but it's gone!

VAL	Oh give up.
RICH	When I look in the mirror I can see my dad.
LEO	We keep active, tha sees!
RICH	That's right!
LEO	Tha's got a woman's job!
RICH	Do you reckon?
LEO	Don't you?
RICH	Well . . . I –
LEO	It's a woman's job, in't it?
RICH	Well . . .
LEO	I mean look at thee hands.
RICH	(*looking at his hands*) Come the revolution!
DANNY	Yeh, they reckon it all drops at forty!
RICH	Some bits drop further than others!
DANNY	I'll look forward to that.
VAL	You're worse than bloody women!
	(RICH *nods towards* VAL'S *prominent bust.*)
RICH	Well it doesn't appear to have affected you, does it?
VAL	Eh?
RICH	Well, I mean . . .
VAL	What?
RICH	I couldn't help but notice!
LEO	What?
RICH	Well . . .

LEO	Argh!
RICH	What?
LEO	You shouldn't be looking . . .
RICH	Well, you know . . .
LEO	What do you reckon then?
RICH	Well, I . . .
LEO	It's usually the first thing anybody says when they meet her . . .
RICH	Well, I didn't know what to say, to be honest.
VAL	He loves it . . .
RICH	I bet he does!
LEO	It's the best money we've ever spent!
VAL	That's what he says.
LEO	We're having it all done . . .
RICH	Yeh?
VAL	Bum, chin everything.
LEO	We're doing her up, aren't we?
VAL	That's what he says –
RICH	Lovely . . .
LEO	Aye we're doing a "Changing Rooms" on her!
RICH	Smashing!
LEO	I was watching your face . . .
RICH	What?
LEO	You couldn't keep your eyes off 'em . . .
RICH	No, man . . .

LEO	Ha haaaa!
	(VICKY *returns from the toilet. She also has a bag of crisps with her.*)
VICKY	They reckon the taxi's have stopped running now!
RICH	What?
VICKY	It's just been on t' tele.
RICH	What?
VICKY	They're blockading . . .
RICH	Oh no!
VICKY	Petrol!
RICH	Again?
VAL	That's it, then.
LEO	That's it, then.
VAL	It could turn into an all-nighter!
RICH	(*to* VICKY) No taxis?
VICKY	Nowt on t' road.
LEO	It's all grinding to a halt.
RICH	Bloody hell!
LEO	It's all going bad.
RICH	Aren't we all right?
LEO	They couldn't organise a piss-up in a brewery!
RICH	You're probably right.
LEO	Bloody rivers, floods . . .
RICH	That's right.

LEO   Petrol, every bloody thing . . . It's all gunna go
             belly up.

RICH   It is tonight!

DANNY   Let's have another drink then, shall we?

VICKY   You what?

DANNY   There's isn't a lot we can do about it!

VICKY   What?

DANNY   (*to* LEO) Are we having another?

LEO   Can do!

VAL   (*to* RICH) You coming down the Rock?

LEO   'Course he is!

RICH   How am I going to get back, though?

LEO   I'll drive you.

RICH   Well, I . . .

LEO   I'll be too drunk to sing anyway!

RICH   No, I'm going to have to go home!

LEO   You said that an hour ago!

RICH   I know.

LEO   And we caught you with that pross!

RICH   Hey no, listen . . .

VICKY   You what?

VAL   Leo caught him with a young lass.

RICH   Hey no, listen here –

VAL   Argh!

RICH   Bloody hell . . .

VAL	Don't worry about it . . .
VICKY	(*to* RICH) Dirty sod . . .
RICH	I'd better give Becky a call . . .
	(RICH *reaches for his mobile.*)
LEO	What for?
RICH	Well if . . . ?
LEO	Bloody leave her, man!
RICH	Yes?
LEO	She's probably letting her hair down.
VAL	It could all be a front, you know?
RICH	What?
VAL	This reunion thing.
RICH	No, I don't –
VAL	It might be some girls' night out!
RICH	I don't –
VAL	Oh, come off it!
RICH	What?
VAL	I wasn't born yesterday.
RICH	Well maybe . . .
VAL	Bloody women are crackers at times.
RICH	Do you reckon?
VAL	They've probably organised a stripper or some Anne Summers' night.
RICH	Well, you never know.
VAL	Let her have a good time.

RICH   (*resigned*) I can't bloody stop her, can I?

          (LEO *becomes effusive*.)

LEO   Hey, I'll tell you sommat, though!

RICH   What?

LEO   Your Sophie.

RICH   What about her?

LEO   Ohhh!

RICH   Yes?

LEO   Oh, man!

RICH   What?

LEO   Lovely.

RICH   Well . . .

LEO   You should see his daughter.

VAL   Yes?

LEO   She's going to make somebody very happy.

RICH   Not tonight I hope.

VAL   You never know.

RICH   That's right –

LEO   You never know.

RICH   That's right.

LEO   She might be gobbling some spotty kid off as
          we speak!

VAL   Leo!

VICKY   You what?

LEO   Well, she might!

(A beat. Tension.)

RICH   Aye, she might.

LEO   I'm not being offensive, am I?

RICH   What?

LEO   I'm not being offensive?

RICH   Course not!

LEO   Oh yes man . . . very nice.

RICH   Thank you!

              (A beat.)

LEO   And your lass!

RICH   Oh yes?

LEO   Oh.

RICH   Yes?

LEO   Posh!

RICH   Well . . .

LEO   Very lardy, isn't she?

RICH   Well . . .

LEO   Smart woman . . . I think so!

LEO   *(to* VAL*)* You should see their lass.

VAL   Yes?

LEO   She's a cracker!

VAL   Lovely.

LEO   *(to* DANNY*)* Classy, isn't she?

DANNY   He scored her well high!

RICH	What?
DANNY	He scored her very high!
RICH	How do you mean?
VAL	This is what they do . . .
RICH	What?
VAL	They say how much they'd have to drink to sleep with somebody.
RICH	(*laughing, but uncomfortable*) Oh, right!
LEO	It's only a joke.
DANNY	It's just sommat to do.
LEO	When we get bored . . .
DANNY	It's only a joke . . .
RICH	That's right.
VAL	I think it's pathetic!
RICH	Yeh?
VAL	I'd have to be pissed to sleep with either of them, wouldn't you?
RICH	Absolutely legless . . .
LEO	Arghh! Nice one!
DANNY	I scored Becky low.
RICH	She'll be gutted!
DANNY	Do you think so?
VICKY	What's he say . . . ?
LEO	So what about Val?
RICH	What?

LEO	Val!
RICH	What?
LEO	How do you score her?
VAL	Don't be soft!
LEO	How much would it take to sleep with her?
RICH	No. I . . .
LEO	Go on . . .
RICH	No . . . I can't . . .
VAL	Leo . . . ?
LEO	It's only a joke . . .
RICH	No, I . . .
LEO	I mean I scored their lass, half a shandy . . .
VAL	Oh, right . . .
LEO	It's only fair he has a shot . . .
RICH	No, honestly . . .
LEO	Chicken . . .
RICH	That's right . . .
LEO	Four pints . . .
RICH	No, listen . . .
LEO	More?
RICH	Probably less, but –
LEO	Oh, hear that?
VICKY	Probably less.
DANNY	Good score, Val . . .
VAL	I should bloody hope so!

RICH	No, I'm –
LEO	What's up wi' thee, dunt tha like her . . . ?
RICH	Well . . .
LEO	She likes thee.
VAL	He's all right.
RICH	Oh, thanks.
VAL	I've seen better.
LEO	What would it take, then?
VAL	Less than four.
VICKY	What's he say?
LEO	I'll tell thee what it takes, shall I?
RICH	Go on . . .
LEO	Pure champagne.
RICH	Very good!
LEO	I'm telling thee. Pure champagne!
VAL	Take no gorm on him, once he's had a drink, he'll say anything!
LEO	(to VAL) I was being flattering!
VAL	Bless him!
LEO	Right, we'll have another here and then get down the Rock.
RICH	I don't know if I'm . . .
VAL	If we go in the back room it'll be quieter.
LEO	Come and listen to some Northern Soul, mate – we'll show you what it's all about, won't we?

VAL	Course we will!
LEO	So are you coming or what?
RICH	Go on, I'll come for a look.
LEO	Argh!
VAL	That's more like it!
	(*Music. Blackout.*)

Scene Ten

The Rock. 11.15 pm.

VAL, LEO, VICKY and DANNY *enter the Rock dance floor. A mirror ball spins, and Northern Soul plays. The four of them immediately begin to dance in a formation, they are all very good.* RICH *stands with a pint by the sideline and watches. They encourage him to dance.*

RICH	Very good!
VAL	Come!
RICH	Very very good . . .
VAL	Come on . . .
RICH	I'm not . . .
VAL	Get on here . . .
	(VAL *goes and grabs* RICH *and brings him onto the dance floor. He begins to dance with them, he can hardly keep the rhythm but then starts to get it, there are whoops of delight as he fits in the routine. During the routine* LEO *launches into a solo spot, then* DANNY *does the same, followed by* VICKY *and finally* VAL, *then* RICH *is encouraged to do a solo dance. He reluctantly steps forward and tries to dance, they all laugh at him. He is pissed and*

slightly out of control. RICH *and* LEO *are together.*)

LEO	Hey, I tell thee sommat . . .
RICH	What?
LEO	When I saw thee this morning . . .
RICH	Yeh?
LEO	I never expected this . . .
RICH	No . . . ?
LEO	I thought tha was a right arsehole . . .
RICH	Yeh?
LEO	Did tha, Danny?
DANNY	Oh, aye.
RICH	I thought the same . . .
LEO	I never expected you being here . . .
RICH	Neither did I, mate . . .
LEO	I mean look at me and him. We're scratching about for a few quid making a living . . .
RICH	That's right . . .
LEO	And look at thee, tha's got a brilliant house.
RICH	Well . . .
LEO	A fucking smart wife . . . sorry pal.
RICH	No problem.
LEO	A gorgeous daughter . . .
RICH	That's right.
LEO	And do you know what?

RICH	What?
LEO	We do the same job!
RICH	We do, don't we?
LEO	(*easily*) Bastard!
RICH	Yeh?
LEO	Bastard . . .
RICH	That's right . . .
LEO	I hate you!

(RICH *recognises a track, which is now playing.*)

RICH	(*to the music*) Hey! I know this.
LEO	What?
RICH	Bloody hell I know this . . . Ha ha, I know this one!

(RICH *starts to dance.* LEO *watches him and finishes his drink.*)

| LEO | Argh! |
| RICH | Come on then . . . what are you waiting for? |

(*They encourage* RICH *to dance with them once more. They strike up a routine, as they progress* RICH *gets better and eventually is easily tuned in, as the music finishes they cheer. Blackout. End of Act One.*)

ACT TWO

Scene One

The Rock. 2.00 am.

Soul music plays. Leo, Val Danny *and* Vicky *are still dancing to a soul track. As the music comes to a close they stop dancing.*

LEO   That's it, then!

VAL   I love it in here when it's empty!

VICKY   Quiet tonight, in't it . . . ?

DANNY   There's still a few in the bar . . .

VAL   They're probably staying away because of the petrol job!

LEO   Where's Nutty Norman got to, has he gone?

VAL   Gone to get another round in . . .

LEO   Does he know what time it is?

VAL   This is his sixth . . .

LEO   I wish he'd stop dancin', he's scaring me to death!

           (*They all laugh at* RICH'S *expense.*)

VAL   He's only trying to fit in . . .

DANNY   I'll tell you sommat, cheap night . . .

VICKY   Aye, he's bought nearly every round.

           (*They laugh again at* RICH'S *expense.*)

LEO   Hey don't you go having too much . . .

VICKY   Don't you . . .

LEO   Don't you worry about me!

               (RICH *enters, he has five bottles of Pils. He
               looks a complete mess, and is dripping with
               sweat. His shirt is stuck to him.*)

RICH   Argh!

VAL   Here he is, look!

RICH   Arghh!

LEO   We thought you'd gone home!

RICH   I'm not going home just yet, don't worry about
               that. Now then, a bottle each, anybody doesn't
               want one, I'll have two!

               (RICH *hands a bottle of beer to each of the
               others.*)

DANNY   Cheers, Rich . . .

RICH   Cheers everybody!

LEO
VAL   }   Cheers!
VICKY

               (*A beat.*)

RICH   Well, here we are . . .

LEO   Cheers, mate!

RICH   (*sings, and does a little dance*) Hey, "Do you
               like soul music? Yeh, Yeh, I said sweet soul
               music?"

LEO   Good night?

RICH   Oh, aye.

VAL   I'll have to pay a call . . .

               (VAL *exits.*)

RICH   Oh man, what a night! (*Sings.*) Oh what a night!

DANNY   Argh man, look at him . . .

RICH   (*sings*) Do you like soul music . . . ?

              (RICH *goes up to* VICKY, *as* LEO *and* DANNY
              attend to their drinks.)

              You all right, then?

VICKY   Not bad!

RICH   Quiet, aren't you?

VICKY   You know what they say?

RICH   What about?

VICKY   Quiet ones . . .

RICH   Oh, right. I was just thinking, you couldn't
              wear much less, could you?

VICKY   You what?

              (RICH *stands silent and simply oogles* VICKY.
              She begins to feel uncomfortable.)

              What, you looking at?

RICH   Your tattoo.

VICKY   Do you like it?

RICH   Oh aye, nice . . . I like body art.

VICKY   I had it done in Brid . . .

RICH   (*feeling her tattoo*) I like tattoos on women.
              Classy.

VICKY   It was only seven quid! You could have a
              tattoo and your stomach pierced for seven
              quid.

(RICH *looks at her tattoo and the rest of her.*)

RICH   There's some good deals about!

VICKY   They did all sorts. I was going to have Chinese writing up my back but he said I'd look like a menu so I left it.

        (RICH *is very close to* VICKY. LEO *doesn't like it, and watches from upstage.*)

RICH   Can I kiss it?

VICKY   What?

RICH   Your tattoo.

VICKY   What for?

RICH   I just want to . . .

VICKY   Can you chuff . . .

RICH   Oh, go on . . .

        (RICH *kisses* VICKY'S *tattoo.*)

DANNY   (*half in jest*) Hey up, what's going off over there?

RICH   I'm just admiring the art work.

DANNY   Go steady . . .

RICH   I'm only having a look.

LEO   You're pissed up!

RICH   Who?

LEO   You!

        (RICH *begins to touch* VICKY *in a half innocent manner.*)

RICH   I'm not bad, I was just having a chat because, we haven't really, you know. (*To* VICKY.) I

haven't offended you, have I? You're not
offended, are you? I didnt mean to . . . you
know?

VICKY   (*to* LEO) He's crackers, in't he?

             (RICH *wanders around the disco with his beer.*)

RICH   Is he going to play any more music, then?

LEO   Not tonight!

RICH   Why not?

LEO   That's it!

RICH   Eh?

LEO   That's it!

RICH   That's it?

LEO   We're going to have this and leg it!

RICH   Oh, this is no good . . . !

VICKY   What?

RICH   I was just getting into it.

VICKY   You should have danced more!

RICH   I would have done but I've been stood at the
             bar half the night getting the bloody drinks in!

LEO   You'll have to come down next week.

             (*Everyone takes a drink.*)

RICH   (*exasperated*) Is that it, really?

VICKY   It's ten past two . . .

LEO   He's only got a license till twelve, we've been
             locked in for two hours!

VICKY   He's that pissed he didn't realise!

RICH   Hey, listen . . .

DANNY   Oh, he's off!

            (*A beat.*)

RICH   So what are we doing, then?

LEO   Eh?

RICH   Are we going on somewhere?

LEO   Where ?

RICH   Where is there?

LEO   Nowhere.

DANNY   There is nowhere!

RICH   Isn't there that drinking club on the docks?

DANNY   Which drinking club?

RICH   It was on the docks: you had to say Fat M had
            sent you and they let you in . . . it was in
            somebody's house, they served you miniatures
            through a hole in the wall, it was full of
            Russians.

LEO   They shut that ten years ago.

            (RICH *swigs at his bottle.*)

RICH   Bloody hell . . . I'm just getting warmed up.

LEO   We should have got down here earlier . . .

RICH   Well why didn't we?

LEO   Well, you didn't want to come for a start!

RICH   (*beginning to shout*) Oh hang on, we can't
            have this! I can't believe that that's it . . . it's
            ridiculous, I mean where are we living? Two
            o'clock and that's it? Bloody Fascists!

            (VICKY *lights up a cigarette.*)

VICKY	I thought you were going home anyway?
RICH	Can't we get him to play a few more? Can't you use your influence?
LEO	I've got none.
	(RICH *wanders upstage and shouts off. This is beginning to aggravate* DANNY *and* LEO.)
RICH	(*begins shouting*) Put some more music on you fascist bastard! Where is he? Danny, go and tell him!
DANNY	I'm not telling him.
RICH	Go and see if he'll play a couple more records and if he doesn't tell him I'll drop him!
LEO	(*matter of fact*) He's only got one arm.
RICH	Tell him I'll break the other!
VICKY	Go on, I'll come wi' you. I want to get some fags.
DANNY	(*leaving*) Two more, I'll ask for.
	(DANNY *and* VICKY *exit.* RICH *and* LEO *stand together in silence.*)
RICH	Oh!
LEO	Yeh.
RICH	Oh, oh! Man ha, ha!
LEO	Oh dear!
	(*A beat.*)
RICH	I say, I can't believe Danny's with Vicky!
LEO	What?
RICH	Oh dear me . . .

LEO	What?
RICH	Dear me!
LEO	Oh, aye.
RICH	She's a right . . .
LEO	Aye . . . well?
RICH	Come on . . .
LEO	What?
RICH	Bloody hell . . .
LEO	What?
	(*A beat.*)
RICH	What do you score her?
LEO	Eh?
RICH	Vicky?
LEO	Well it's Danny's wife, in't it . . .
	(*A beat.*)
RICH	I've got her well up.
LEO	Yes . . . ?
RICH	A *very* good score . . .
LEO	Have you?
RICH	Oh aye, I've scored her very high . . . mind you, bloody hell!
LEO	What?
RICH	What's she wearing?
LEO	(*stoical*) That's right.

RICH   Listen, I don't know what standards you lads
              work from but I've got her down as a glass of
              Claret and a cream egg!

LEO   Have you?

RICH   And listen, if I was pushed I'd do without the
              cream egg!

LEO   Would you?

RICH   If I was really pushed I'd probably do without
              the claret . . . oh dear!

              (*A beat.*)

LEO   Cool off, man!

RICH   What?

LEO   Cool off!

RICH   Cool off . . . I can't cool off. I'm wet through,
              it's pissing out of me . . . I've not been to the
              bog all night, I haven't needed to it's coming
              out of my forehead.

              (DANNY, VICKY *and* VAL *re-enter.*)

DANNY   He says he'll play one more.

RICH   (*sings*) "Do you like soul music?"

VAL   So get dancing, you . . .

RICH   (*singing*) "Do you like soul music?"

              (*Music: Long After Tonight Is All Over, a
              Northern classic.* RICH *begins to dance
              straight away. He grabs* VAL *and she is forced
              to dance as well.* VICKY *dances and smokes.*)

RICH   Come on . . .

VAL   Oh heck . . .

RICH   Come on, let's see you bounce about a bit . . .

VAL	Hey . . .
RICH	Well . . .
VAL	I'm a married woman . . .
RICH	I'm a married man . . .

(RICH, VAL *and* VICKY *dance.* LEO *and* DANNY *drift down to the corner of the dance floor.*)

LEO	So where did you learn to dance, then?
RICH	It's in my blood, mate!
LEO	I thought you said you didn't know any Northern?
RICH	It was years ago . . . !
DANNY	This is main stream stuff, everybody knows it.
RICH	Don't he defensive, man.
DANNY	I'm not being!
RICH	Come on, get on here, we could be here all night!
LEO	No. We've got to go home, we're up early tomorrow doing some tosser's house up!
RICH	Forget it, he'll probably not pay you anyway.
LEO	I bloody hope so . . .
RICH	Come on, get on here, what's up with you?
LEO	All right . . .

(*Music.* RICH *picks up the beat* . . . LEO *starts to dance, so does* DANNY, VAL *and* VICKY. LEO *dances as a kind of threat to* RICH.)

RICH	Oh, ho . . . come on, then . . . !

(*Music swells. Blackout.*)

Scene Two

The marina. 2.35 am.

*The marina has a number of seats and litter bins. It is dark
and cold.* DANNY *and* LEO *enter, they have a hot dog each.
Both are not drunk, but loose and dangerous.*

LEO	Bloody hell, it's cold out here . . .
DANNY	Freezing . . .
LEO	I love it on the marina, though . . .
DANNY	Where's he gone?
LEO	(*eating*) To get some more sauce . . .
DANNY	I thought he wa' gunna get nutted, what was he on about?
LEO	(*eating*) He was still complaining about the drinking hours to that copper!
DANNY	(*enjoying it*) He should've gone home . . .
LEO	He's all right, just a bit of an arse . . .
DANNY	They all are though, aren't they?
LEO	How do you mean?
DANNY	(*eating*) Them with money! What about that twat in Willerby who kept them fish? Every day we went he showed us his fish, didn't he? He had all different names for 'em, can you remember?
LEO	(*eating*) Nice bloke!
DANNY	(*eating*) I ended up nicking one – do you remember? A big fuckin' Koi! Stuck it on the front of the van!
	(*A beat.*)

LEO   Where are they?

DANNY   Vicky's having another pee . . . Val's gone with
           her.

LEO   Why do they allus go together?

DANNY   It's a mystery, in't it?

           (*A beat.*)

LEO   Is Vicky all right . . . she seems a bit . . . ?

DANNY   No, she's all right . . .

LEO   (*eating*) That's all right, then!

           (*A beat, as they eat their hot dogs.*)

DANNY   I'm not . . .

LEO   What?

DANNY   All right . . .

LEO   Why?

DANNY   I dunno . . .

LEO   What's up?

DANNY   Well . . .

           (LEO *looks dangerously at* DANNY.)

LEO   (*disappointed*) Oh, I knew you'd do this . . .

DANNY   What?

LEO   Don't let me down!

DANNY   Have I ever?

LEO   Not yet.

           (*A beat.*)

DANNY	So are we still on, then?
LEO	Course we are . . . we'll get straight back and get settled!
DANNY	Oh right . . . What about Nutty?
LEO	Well we'll dump him, won't we?
DANNY	Will we?
LEO	How do you mean?
DANNY	Well I think we've got a friend for life . . .
	(*The atmosphere is tense when* RICH *enters with a hot dog.*)
RICH	Copper back there says there's no taxis running! It's all gone belly up, he says! There's no taxis, there's no buses.
DANNY	(*eating*) And the trains are fucked anyway, so you're knackered!
RICH	(*eating*) Lovely!
LEO	Stranded, then.
RICH	He did say he'd run me home for three hundred quid, but . . .
DANNY	(*eating*) You can always trust a policeman!
RICH	(*eating*) I tried to bargain him down but he wasn't having any of it! He says there's thousands of pissed-up people walking home in the middle of the road! It's like 'The Dawn of the Dead', he says! He's a good bloke actually, I had quite a laugh with him!
DANNY	Can't you sleep in his car?
RICH	(*eating*) No. There's two in there already!
LEO	So you're comin' with me?

RICH	Well you can't leave me, can you?
DANNY	Can't we?
LEO	I mean I'll drop you off, but are you sure you can't drive yourself?
RICH	I can't even remember where I parked!
LEO	You parked by the Chinese.
RICH	It was four days ago . . .
LEO	It wasn't.
RICH	(*eating*) It bloody feels like it.
	(*A beat.*)
LEO	Enjoyed it, then?
RICH	Oh, aye!
LEO	I thought so . . .
RICH	It's funny though, isn't it?
LEO	What?
RICH	You always think you're going to score, don't you?
LEO	How do you mean?
RICH	I mean no matter how much of an absolute outside chance it is, you always think you're going to get off with somebody!
LEO	Argh!
RICH	Even at forty-five . . . bloody hell, it's a curse!
LEO	(*laughing*) So did you?
RICH	Well I wasn't trying to, was I?
LEO	So, if you'd've tried you would have?

DANNY   Here we go . . .

RICH   Listen mate, I can't score in an open goal. I'm
             not saying that, I'm saying the thoughts are
             still there.

             (VICKY *and* VAL *enter.* VAL *can now start
             eating her hot dog.*)

VAL   (*to* VICKY) Mine's gone cold – you take that
             long . . .

VICKY   I've got to go . . . !

VAL   I thought you were flooding us!

VICKY   I can't hold it like I could . . .

             (*They arrive at the men.*)

VAL   So what's happening then?

             (LEO *puts his hot dog wrapper in a bin.*)

LEO   We're going to get off!

RICH   There's no taxis running at all.

VAL   Are you OK to drive?

LEO   Who?

VAL   You!

LEO   I've driven worse than this. Anyway there'll be
             nowt on the road.

RICH   (*walking away*) Only the police!

             (RICH *finishes his hot dog, and puts his
             wrapper in the bin . Sings: "Hey Jimmy, oh
             Jimmy Mack, when are you coming back?"*)

VAL   You enjoyed it, then?

RICH   Oh, a good night!

VAL	A very good night!
RICH	(*sings*) "At last my dream come through, today he said I do!" I'm going to buy some of that stuff! (*Sings*.) "Long after tonight is all over, long after tonight is all gone . . ." What is it?
VAL	(*shivering*) God it's freezing out here!
	(RICH *is slightly away from the other group*.)
LEO	We'll drop him off and then we'll get back.
VAL	I've got some stuff in, so . . .
LEO	We'll have to take it steady, that's all! Is that still all right with you, Vick?
VICKY	(*dreamily*) Yeh, I'm all right . . .
VAL	She's all right, we've had a –
	(RICH *suddenly is filled with life*.)
RICH	Well why don't you come back to mine?
LEO	You what?
RICH	Why don't you come back to mine, and let's try and keep it going?
LEO	No mate, thanks but –
RICH	Oh!
LEO	What?
RICH	Oh, man!
LEO	What?
RICH	Party pooper!
LEO	No, listen . . .
RICH	Oh! I thought you knew how to live? Come on, man?

LEO   No! Val?

RICH   Listen, I've got some beer in, we can have
           another drink, put some sounds on . . . Yes,
           come on! We can't hurt anything, the house is
           a tip in anyway!

LEO   What's tha reckon, Dan?

DANNY   I'm easy.

VAL   It's just that, weve got some stuff laid on, kid.

RICH   Don't worry about that, we've got everything
           you need. Quiche, sausage rolls, there's some
           ham and all. Becky's left some cookies, we've
           even got them oat cakes that fucking Prince
           Charles has! Have you had them with a bit of
           Brie? Oh man, come on . . . (*Shouting.*) . . .
           Yeah . . . now! (*Sings.*) "Do you like soul
           music?" Come on now! Now! (*Histrionic.*) Yes!
           Come to the pleasure dome . . . Yes, everybody
           now . . .

           (*A beat.*)

LEO   Go on then, we'll have one!

RICH   (*pleased, and slightly deranged*) Arghh!

           (*Music. Blackout.*)

                       Scene Three

Living room. 2.50 am.

*Through the blackout a number of large dust sheets have been
brought on stage by the cast in a dance like sequence. These
dust sheets cover the existing furniture which formed the set
for the Marina scene. Other pieces of furniture are also
brought into the space to give the sense of being in* RICH'S
living room. There are a number of photos on the wall. One of
BECKY *in swim wear, another of* BECKY, SOPHIE *and* RICH *at a
school awards evening. There is also a music centre and a*

number of CDs inside it, this is covered by a dust sheet. There are also some ladders and pots of paint randomly laid about the room. VICKY, VAL, RICH, DANNY *and* LEO *enter from upstage. There is a real sense of respect at this time for the space. All speak in hushed tones to start with.*

RICH   Come in, come in, come in!

VAL   Oh it's lovely, isn't it?

RICH   Sit down.

VAL   Isn't it?

RICH   Make yourself at home. I'll just make a call . . .

            (RICH *exits.*)

VAL   Nice, isn't it?

LEO   Told you, didn't I?

VAL   Lovely, isn't it? What do you think, Vicky?

VICKY   (*sullen*) S'all right!

            (VAL *and* VICKY *make themselves comfortable.* LEO *and* DANNY *move around the room menacingly. They look at the photos on the wall.*)

LEO   That's their lass, Val. I say, that's their lass. Nice, isn't she?

DANNY   Posh, isn't she?

VAL   Oh, like me then . . .

LEO   (*looking at the photo*) Smart on that . . .

            (LEO *moves to another photo and picks it up.*)

            This is the daughter . . .

VAL   Oh . . . young, then!

LEO   You can't really see her on that one, but . . .

VAL	(*looking around*) Oh aye, it's going to be nice!
LEO	Right, shall we get started then?
VAL	What's he like?
LEO	Good place for it though, nice and private.
	(RICH *enters with a variety of different drinks.*)
RICH	Beer, brandy, what?
LEO	Beer.
VAL	Brandy.
DANNY	What?
RICH	Vicky?
VICKY	I'll have a brandy, cock. Can we smoke?
RICH	Aye go on then, this is usually a non-smoking house but . . . since I like your tattoo, you can do what you want.
VAL	Sounds like you're in there, Vicky.
VICKY	I know, he's all over my tattoo, aren't you?
RICH	I love good art.
VICKY	Bullshitter.
RICH	I've bullshitted with the best of 'em, kid!
VAL	Absolutely.
LEO	Gunna put some music on, then?
RICH	Aye, put some on, under there somewhere. I'll go and get a few glasses.
	(RICH *exits.* LEO *and* DANNY *drift over to the music centre.*)
LEO	(*shouts*) Got any Northern?

RICH *re-appears in the alcove.*)

RICH	Oh aye, I've got loads . . . Jimmy Saville, Geoff Boycott . . . Darren Gough!
LEO	Oh . . . aye.
RICH	Well, they're all Northern! There's all sorts in there, just stick something on.

(RICH *disappears off stage.* LEO *moves over to the music centre and starts to select through a range of CDs.*)

VAL	Nice and big, isn't it?
DANNY	Four bedrooms, all en-suite and all!
VICKY	You've been through it, have you?
DANNY	What do you think we are?
LEO	(*looking through CDs*) Don't answer that!
VAL	Nice.
LEO	(*selecting*) Got some brilliant stuff in his study, hasn't he, Dan?
DANNY	Oh, aye.
LEO	(*grabbing a CD*) Here you are . . . "Music to relax to".
VAL	Don't put that on . . . we'll all be asleep.
LEO	Songs of the Mountains . . . Pan Pipe experience?
VAL	No chance!
VICKY	Oh God!
LEO	Leo Sayer!
VICKY	You what?

LEO   The Eagles?

VICKY   The what? Chuffin' hell . . . how old is he?

            (*A beat.*)

VAL   You all right, Dan?

DANNY   Oh, aye.

LEO   (*standing*) Listen, we'll just have one here and
            then we'll get back to ours. Unless anybody
            wants to get started?

VICKY   I'm easy . . .

LEO   That all right. Dan?

DANNY   Well, we can stop here all night for me.

VAL   That'd be different. What about Rich, though?

LEO   Well he's not bringing much to the party, is
            he?

VAL   Only the house!

DANNY   We can't, can we?

VAL   He's joking . . . aren't you?

            (*Some nervous laughter.* LEO *moves from the
            music centre.*)

LEO   Thee find sommat Dan, I can't see 'owt worth
            playing.

DANNY   Let's have a look at what he's got, 'cos tha's
            got no taste.

LEO   In what?

DANNY   Anything!

VAL   Big, isn't it?

LEO   I told you!

(DANNY *crosses to the music centre and looks through some CDs . . . He holds one aloft.*)

DANNY   What about this . . . Edith Piaf?

VICKY   Who?

DANNY   (*not sure*) Is it Piaf ?

VICKY   God knows . . .

VAL   Just put sommat on!

(DANNY *puts on the CD. They all listen to it play.* DANNY *starts to try to dance to it.*)

DANNY   Well you can't dance to it . . .

(*They all laugh.*)

Hey, no . . . listen . . .

(*They all listen and then* DANNY *begins to mime to the music and dance in a surreal mickey-take of the style.*)

LEO   Oh, right . . .

DANNY   I quite like it . . .

VICKY   You what?

DANNY   Oh aye . . . I'm getting this album.

(DANNY *begins to dance around. As he does* RICH *enters. He has a brandy glass and some other bits.*)

LEO   What's this shite, then?

RICH   Great, isn't it?

VAL   Good grief . . .

DANNY   Is she in agony?

LEO   Music to slit your throat to . . .

RICH   Anybody want any eats?

VICKY   Not me! I feel a bit gippy to be honest.

LEO   You haven't got any dope, have you?

RICH   Not me.

LEO   Thought you might have had a conservatory full of it.

RICH   Sorry . . .

LEO   I thought that's what you'd brought us back for?

RICH   Best I can do is a can of Becks.

LEO   It'll have to do!

DANNY   (*to the music*) What is this?

RICH   Piaf . . .

DANNY   Hey man, I like it!

LEO   It's shite . . .

RICH   Beer, brandy, what?

VAL   Turn it off Danny, it'll give me a bloody migraine!

DANNY   I don't mind it.

            (DANNY *flicks the hand console to off.* RICH *hands out the respective drinks.*)

VAL   How much is it worth, then?

RICH   The house?

LEO   Three hundred and fifty!

RICH   No!

LEO	Easily . . . there's one in Kirkella for two-fifty and it's not got half the garden.
RICH	Well, we bought it for one-eight-five.
VICKY	Thousand?
LEO	All that money, and he's only a painter, just like us, you know?
RICH	That's right!
LEO	Bastard!
RICH	Arghh!
LEO	What's ours worth, Val?
VAL	Thirty-seven.
RICH	Well, we've got two wages, Becky's got her . . .
	(LEO *walks over and inspects the photo of* BECKY *once more.*)
LEO	Aye, she looks good on the wall, mate.
RICH	Oh right, that . . .
LEO	Where's this?
RICH	Puerto Banus.
LEO	Nice!
DANNY	We did some stuff down there, didn't we?
RICH	Did you?
LEO	(*looking at the photo*) Aye, we're international us, you know?
VAL	They did some of the Dome, didn't you?
LEO	(*looking at the photo*) I think the less said about that the better. They were all there before the opening. It was like Dunkirk, mate!

RICH   Yes, that's Puerto Banus.

LEO   Looks good with a tan.

RICH   It was boiling that year.

LEO   Aye, she looks good . . .

          (*A beat.*)

RICH   Well, like I say, we've got two wages . . .

LEO   Like us . . .

RICH   Oh right, I didn't know . . .

LEO   Val works.

RICH   That's right, does the books, you said!

LEO   Well, that and all.

RICH   What else does she do, then?

LEO   Didn't she tell you?

RICH   Well she might have done, but –

LEO   You were so chatty, I thought she must have
          told you.

VAL   No, I do have some mystery left, you know?

RICH   Why, what is it?

LEO   Tell him.

VAL   You tell him.

          (*A beat.*)

LEO   No.

RICH   Oh come on, you've got to tell me now!

LEO   Shall I?

VAL	If it'll make you feel better!
LEO	She does these chat lines . . .
RICH	Eh?
LEO	Chat lines. Phone things . . .
	(*A beat.*)
RICH	Oh, right . . .
VAL	So not so shocking, eh?
RICH	Well, somebody's got to do 'em.
LEO	Would your Becky, though?
RICH	(*laughing*) You'd have to ask her.
DANNY	Good money, isn't it Val? (*To* RICH.) She tried to get Vicky on it but she wasn't any good, was you cock?
VICKY	I couldn't think of what to say.
RICH	Don't they read it from a card?
VAL	Well, I don't.
VICKY	I couldn't though, they used to ring up and I thought, well, what shall I say?
RICH	Like you said, the quiet type.
LEO	Aye she's that thick she even told them her real name.
VICKY	Get away, I only did it twice.
LEO	What's your name, Val? Nikita, isn't it?
VAL	Oh aye, I'm a Russian, I'm a size eight and I'm only twenty-one!
LEO	You should hear her!
VAL	It's not bad money.

RICH	Whatever floats your boat.
LEO	You should hear her at times. Do it. Do some of it!
VAL	I'm not doing it here, you soft git!
LEO	I tell you, how she does it in thirty seconds is a work of art.
RICH	I bet it is!
LEO	Go and phone up, you've got to hear her do it!
RICH	Nah . . .
LEO	No, go on, you should hear her, she's brilliant.
VAL	I'm not doing it here!
LEO	She should been on *Stars in Their Eyes*.
VICKY	What as?
LEO	Well . . . sommat.
RICH	Service industries, eh?
LEO	I tell you sommat, she's on the phone sometimes, and I get embarrassed with what she's coming out with.
VAL	Leave it!
LEO	If I'm cooking I can't concentrate on my omelettes.
RICH	Well, there you go . . .
	(*Laughter falls to silence. Everyone begins to relax. All drink and* LEO *sits on the sofa near to* VICKY.)
LEO	Aye well, this is more like it. Isn't it?
VICKY	Yep!

LEO	Nice and relaxing in here.
RICH	Aye, it's a nice room, this.
VAL	Great view, I bet.
RICH	Becky does the garden.
LEO	Yes this is nice in here! Good beer, shit music!
RICH	No taste, mate.
LEO	Well, you can't dance to it.
RICH	Put something else on.
	(*A beat.*)
LEO	Perfect in here though, Richard. Going to be when we finish it.
DANNY	*If* we finish it . . .
	(*Laughter.*)
RICH	Well, cheers everyone!
VAL	Cheers.
DANNY	Cheers.
VICKY	Cheers.
RICH	A very good night.
LEO	Cheers mate. Get a film on and we're laughing.
VICKY	Oh yeh, what have you got?
LEO	And I hope your film taste is better than your music.
RICH	A film?
VAL	Get one on . . .
VICKY	Have you got some?

RICH	I've got *Titanic*.
VICKY	I've not seen that.
DANNY	You know what happens though, don't you?
VICKY	No . . . what?
RICH	We bought it last Christmas and we never watched it.
VAL	They haven't had the time!
RICH	(*laughing*) That's about right!
LEO	Bloody hell, we'll be here all night!
RICH	Erm what else . . . ?
LEO	Haven't you got anything a bit . . .
RICH	What?
LEO	Well . . .
RICH	What?
	(*A beat.*)
LEO	Well, I mean we're all adults, aren't we?
RICH	Oh, you mean a . . . ?
LEO	Get it slapped on . . .
RICH	No, I've got nothing like . . . I've got *Sister Act*. What else . . .
VAL	(*saucy*) Oh, sounds good!
RICH	I've got *Fatal Attraction* . . .
VAL	Michael Douglas . . .
RICH	What else?
DANNY	What about that one upstairs?

(A beat.)

RICH   Eh?

DANNY   There's one upstairs . . .

RICH   Where?

DANNY   There's one in your bedroom.

RICH   Eh?

DANNY   That video in your bedroom. I thought it
            looked a bit –

RICH   Which one's that, then?

DANNY   I dunno, I saw it this morning, just a tape in no
            box or anything. It was at the bottom of that
            wardrobe.

RICH   When did you see that?

DANNY   I was looking for your phone line because –

RICH   In my bedroom?

DANNY   Hey, I wasn't . . . I just open the door –

RICH   In my wardrobe . . . bloody hell, Danny mate –

DANNY   I was looking for the phone box!

LEO   Go and get it!

RICH   Hey, hang on . . .

VICKY   We're not watching another porn film, are we
            Danny?

RICH   I don't even know what it's doing there.

LEO   Argh!

RICH   Hey, honest!

LEO   Argh! Who is it, you and Becky, eh?

RICH   Hey seriously, I've no idea.

LEO   Go and get it, Danny!

RICH   Hey . . . hang on.

DANNY   No, I'd better not.

LEO   (*strong*) Go and get it . . .

            (DANNY *is out of the room very quickly.*)

RICH   Hey, hang on!

LEO   What is it, a home movie?

RICH   What's he been doing going in our bedrooms?

LEO   Hey, hey . . . hang on . . . It's all innocent!

RICH   Is it?

LEO   He panicked when he took the line down . . .

RICH   Well fair enough, but –

LEO   Looks like we've come to the right house,
            anyway!

VAL   Blushing now, aren't you?

RICH   I haven't seen that video for years.

LEO   Oh, here we go . . .

RICH   No seriously, I was doing some paintings from –

VAL   Oh, any excuse . . .

RICH   Please yourself . . .

LEO   Argh!

RICH   I don't even know how it's got there . . . I
            thought I'd thrown them all away!

VAL   Unless Becky's been watching it!

LEO	Or your young 'un?
	(DANNY *re-appears with a video*.)
DANNY	It's here, look!
LEO	Get it on . . .
RICH	Oh, hey, now, hang on . . .
LEO	What's up?
RICH	Well, you know . . .
LEO	What?
RICH	Well no, I don't think –
VAL	What is it, a home movie?
RICH	Hey no, fair's fair, I don't think it's . . . I'm not comfortable with it.
DANNY	I bet you were comfortable making it.
RICH	It's not a home movie, I can assure you!
	(*They all laugh*.)
VICKY	Put it on, let's have a look.
LEO	Yes come on, we'll all consenting –
RICH	Well I'm not.
LEO	Agrh.
	(RICH *snatches the video from* DANNY.)
RICH	(*shouting*) I said *no* . . .
	(*Silence*.)
	Sorry, but fair's fair.
VAL	Oh right!
RICH	Now, fair's fair!

(*A beat.*)

LEO   Fair enough.

RICH   No honest – I feel, a bit, you know . . . ?

           (*A beat.*)

VAL   Oh put it on, I bet it's nowt we haven't seen
           before.

VICKY   Is it animals? I can't stand that!

RICH   I don't know what it is . . .

DANNY   Put it on then, and let's have a look!

RICH   I don't know what the hell you were doing in
           my bedroom, to be honest.

DANNY   Like I said, I just opened the cupboard had a
           look and noticed that!

VICKY   I mean I don't mind people doing it with
           animals but I mean what kind of pervert films
           'em at it?

           (*A beat.*)

LEO   Slap it on!

RICH   No, honestly . . .

           (*A beat.* RICH *puts the video on the floor
           upstage.*)

LEO   Could have been sommat to get us in the mood!

RICH   Sorry.

LEO   Have you got another beer, then?

VAL   Leo . . . ?

LEO   Danny can drive.

VICKY   He can't drive, he's on them tablets, he's not even supposed to drink!

DANNY   I can have one.

VAL   He's had about five.

DANNY   It's just that my nerves get a bit . . .

           (*A beat.*)

RICH   Any one else want another drink?

LEO   Shame about the video.

RICH   Maybe another time.

LEO   I'll take you up on that.

RICH   Listen, if you're that keen you can have it. Take it with you!

LEO   We might do that . . .

RICH   I'm serious . . . I have no . . . use for . . .

VAL   Can I use your loo, kidda . . . ?

           (VAL *stands and makes her way to exit.*)

LEO   Bottom of the stairs . . .

RICH   Yeh, just –

VAL   Isn't it a lovely house?

           (VAL *exits.*)

VICKY   Don't be long, because I need to –

DANNY   There's two upstairs.

RICH   Oh aye . . . straight to the top –

LEO   Bear left . . .

RICH   That's right!

VICKY

I'll probably get lost knowing me . . . It's lovely
and warm, isn't it? It's freezing in our house at
this time of the night, isn't it?

(VICKY *stands and as she makes her way to
depart, she slips slightly*.)

LEO

Are you all right?

VICKY

I think it must have been that brandy! God,
look at me, I'm pathetic!

(VICKY *exits. There is silence amongst the
men*.)

LEO

Look at his face!

RICH

What?

LEO

Don't worry about it!

(*A beat*.)

RICH

No, no, its just with the women, I feel a bit . . .

LEO

Embarrassed?

RICH

Well . . . it's . . .

LEO

We know all about you now, don't we?

RICH

How do you mean?

LEO

Dark bloody horse, mate . . . blue films . . .

RICH

I thought you were broad minded mate, sorry
about that.

LEO

Oh ho . . . !

DANNY

Listen to him . . .

LEO

Absolutely, he was trying to knob some lass
off the street when we saw him.

DANNY

When?

RICH	No, hey –
DANNY	When was this?
LEO	Tonight . . . a right spook, she was!
RICH	I haven't seen that film for ten years, maybe longer.
DANNY	Get it on then . . .
	(*A beat.*)
LEO	Good night though, eh?
RICH	That's right!
LEO	Over too quick for you, wasn't it?
RICH	Well, I was just getting into the dancing.
LEO	It's not over yet.
RICH	Well, the dancing is!
LEO	Oh aye, the dancing is . . .
	(*A beat.*)
DANNY	Nice in here though, Richard mate, well it will be when we finish it. What colour is she having it?
RICH	Marble . . . with gold.
DANNY	Osbourne and Little paper, isn't it? Bloody hell man, top stuff.
RICH	Supposed to be . . .
DANNY	Oh aye, it'll go on these walls a dream . . . We'll need to skim 'em, but . . .
	(*A beat.*)
LEO	Right, then.
DANNY	What?

LEO   I think I'm going to go up.

DANNY   Eh?

LEO   I'm just going to nip up.

RICH   Vicky's on that one, you'll have to use the
           spare room!

LEO   You all right with that?

DANNY   I thought we were going?

LEO   Well?

DANNY   What?

LEO   I'll just nip up and have a look . . . It's OK,
           isn't it?

RICH   What?

LEO   Is it OK if we use the upstairs?

           (*A beat.*)

RICH   What for?

LEO   Well . . .

RICH   What?

LEO   Well, Vicky's gone up there, so . . .

RICH   What?

LEO   Come on . . .

RICH   What?

LEO   Hey, don't give me that . . .

RICH   What?

LEO   You said so yourself about Vicky, and that was
           behind Dan's back.

RICH   What are you on about?

LEO	We can use Sophie's room.
RICH	Eh?
LEO	We'll be all right in there.
RICH	Wow!
LEO	Then we'll not disturb owt for you and Becky, will we?
RICH	Eh, listen!
LEO	I mean, everybody seems to be chilling here so . . .

(LEO *stands to move.* RICH *moves to stop him.*)

RICH	Hey, wait on . . .
LEO	What?
RICH	We're not having that.
LEO	What?
RICH	Just doing that.
LEO	What?
RICH	Where do you think you are?
LEO	We won't hurt owt.
RICH	I'm not bothered.
LEO	He's good for it, aren't you?
DANNY	Well aye, but . . .
RICH	Wow, wow, we're not having that!

(RICH *touches* LEO. LEO *doesn't like it.*)

LEO	Hey, steady mate . . .

(*A beat.*)

RICH   You know, I think you'd better go!

LEO   What?

RICH   I think you'd better go.

LEO   Oh, give up, man!

RICH   I'm serious. I think you'd better go!

LEO   (*to* DANNY) Have you heard him, what's he like?

RICH   Hey, listen!

LEO   He wanted to party an hour ago, now he thinks he's Francis of Assisi.

RICH   Hey mate, I'm serious!

LEO   So am I!

RICH   Hey, listen!

            (RICH *touches* LEO, LEO *stops and looks at him.*)

LEO   Don't touch me!

RICH   I think you'd better go . . .

LEO   Don't touch me like that, Richard.

RICH   I'm serious here . . .

LEO   I'm serious and all.

RICH   Look . . . I think you'd . . .

LEO   Don't ever touch me like that. All right?

RICH   Well . . .

LEO   *All right?*

            (*A beat.*)

RICH   Yes, right, I'm sorry.

LEO	I'll fucking eat you, all right?
RICH	Hey, listen though . . .
LEO	Now don't spoil a good night! Val'll be back in a minute, Danny, so you two can use the spare room. Is that all right?
RICH	If you have to . . .
LEO	There's some Johnnies in the right hand drawer. (*To* RICH.) Who were you saving them for, then?
RICH	Hey now, listen . . .
LEO	It's nowt, don't worry about it . . . everybody on this street is doing it. Told you that you were living the wrong life, didn't we?
	(LEO *exits. Silence.* RICH *is visibly shaken.* DANNY *snaps on another Piaf track, which plays under. Silence.* DANNY *stands listening to Piaf.*)
RICH	Did you know about this?
	(*A beat.*)
DANNY	Not bad once you've listened to this, is it?
RICH	Did you know about this?
DANNY	Good, isn't it?
	(*A beat.*)
RICH	So is it a regular . . . ?
DANNY	It is with them . . . We've never done it before.
	(*A beat.*)
RICH	Bloody hell.
DANNY	I know.

RICH   I mean . . .

DANNY   He's been on about it for ages. Listen, don't
            get me wrong, I'm not into it, it's just that I've
            got to work with him. I kept saying no but he
            just kept going fucking on about it!

RICH   It's your wife, though?

DANNY   That's the whole point, isn't it?

RICH   So wasn't she . . . ?

DANNY   I dunno. I mean, I think it's just sommat
            different, but you don't know our Leo, he's
            fucking crackers! Once he gets an idea he
            keeps going on about it. Everybody in the
            family are scared shitless of him, I mean you
            never know which way he's gonna jump!

RICH   So it's going to be you and Val, then?

DANNY   Hey, listen . . .

RICH   Bloody hell!

DANNY   I know . . . all that meat and no veg!

            (VAL *enters.*)

VAL   Lovely toilet, that one downstairs, I was just
            reading that *Hello!* Looks like Melanie Griffiths
            has got a tattoo, just like Vicky's . . . Lovely in
            there! Like being in a hotel . . . She's got
            good taste, hasn't she? That Crabtree and
            Evelyn's supposed to be good stuff and all. I
            tried a bit, hope she won't mind.

RICH   No, I don't suppose a bit of perfume will make
            much of a difference.

VAL   That's what I thought.

RICH   It looks like you've tried everything else.

            (*A beat.* VAL *looks around the room.*)

VAL   It's lovely in there, isn't it?

           (*A beat.*)

           Has Leo gone up . . . ?

RICH   Oh aye, he's gone up.

VAL   Oh, right. I thought he was joking.

RICH   Like shit off a shovel. He's gone up. I mean, I
           don't know what he's doing but he's gone up!

           (VAL *reclines in the sofa.*)

VAL   So, here we are, then . . .

RICH   That's right.

VAL   Here we are . . .

RICH   Too right.

           (*A beat.*)

VAL   Just the three of us!

RICH   Eh?

VAL   I said just the three of us!

RICH   Hey, hang on a minute . . .

VAL   How do you feel about that, Dan?

DANNY   Well . . .

RICH   What?

VAL   (*apologetic*) I didn't know Leo had gone up –
           you should have given me a shout, love! We
           can take our time, you know? I mean, there's no
           need to rush, we're cosy just sat here, aren't
           we?

RICH   Aren't we just?

DANNY   I'm not, you know . . .

VAL	What?
DANNY	Well . . . you know?
VAL	You don't have to actually do anything if you don't want, you know.
DANNY	Well, that's . . .
VAL	I mean, you can just watch if you want.
DANNY	Watch . . .
RICH	Watch what?
VAL	Well . . .
RICH	Hey, hang on, I think there's been a –
VAL	I mean you can leave it all to me if you want.
	(*A beat.*)
DANNY	I think I'll go and get a breath of fresh air. Is there another beer, mate?
RICH	In the fridge, kid.
DANNY	I'll just nip and –
VAL	Are you coming back?
DANNY	(*stands*) Give me a knock when our Leo's done, I'll be in the garden.
	(DANNY *sheepishly leaves. Silence.*)
VAL	(*caring*) Oh!
RICH	What?
VAL	First timer.
RICH	So he said.
VAL	There's a lot like that . . .

RICH   I bet there is . . .

            (*A beat.*)

VAL   Going to be lovely in the kitchen. I had a bit of
            a nosey. Big American fridge and all! And are
            they your paintings under the stairs?

RICH   That's right!

VAL   Good, aren't they? One of them looks like the
            earth and it's all covered in cow mess.

RICH   That's about right!

VAL   Weird, that!

RICH   Do you think so?

            (*A beat.*)

VAL   I didn't know that Leo had started . . . I mean
            usually it's only fair to have the same time.

RICH   Oh aye, that seems fair.

VAL   Shocked, are you?

RICH   That it's happening in my house, probably!

VAL   He's been trying to talk Danny but
            I mean, I'm not going to eat him, am I?

RICH   Well, I'm not a prude, but . . .

VAL   Oh, you are!

RICH   You reckon?

VAL   Well what about the film, we could get it on
            now, me and you!

            (*A beat.*)

RICH   Maybe I am, now you come to mention it!

            (*A beat.*)

VAL   He shouldn't hurt anything anyway!

RICH   It's not that . . .

VAL   You probably have cleaners anyway, don't
             you?

RICH   What's he going to do?

VAL   Oh no, don't worry, I mean he's . . .

RICH   What? Crackers . . . ?

VAL   No, there's no problem with Leo.

RICH   Depends what you're talking about, doesn't it?

VAL   Well he's firing blanks anyway. So there's no
             worry there.

RICH   Oh . . . right.

             (*A beat.*)

VAL   Funny, isn't it?

RICH   Do you think?

VAL   I mean, you wouldn't think it to look at him,
             would you?

RICH   It was the last thing on my mind when he came
             this morning, to be honest!

VAL   We did try and have all the stuff, but . . .

             (*A beat.* RICH *drinks.*)

RICH   I'm surprised you couldn't find somebody to
             help out?

VAL   Oh no, he's a bit funny at times, with the other
             men.

RICH   Is he?

VAL	Oh aye, he's quite competitive. I mean I don't mind, but I think he likes the idea of him doing it more than me doing it, do you follow me?
RICH	I do, I do.
VAL	Because he never wants to know about my side.
RICH	No, right, well, fair enough!
VAL	Don't get me wrong, we haven't been doing it that long anyway, only this last two years. That's why we went for all this stuff!
	(VAL *refers to her bust.*)
RICH	Right!
VAL	Well they reckon kids keep you young, and we're not having any, so I thought, if we're not, I'll try and keep, you know, my shape and work it like that. So Leo suggested, you know, when things started to go downhill. Downhill, have you heard me? So that's how . . .
RICH	Well, there you go!
VAL	Well I haven't put a pound on in the last five years! I try and keep in shape.
RICH	I wish I could say that!
	(*A beat.*)
VAL	Lovely in here, though . . .
RICH	Yeah!
VAL	Lovely in here . . .
RICH	It will be . . .
	(*A beat.*)
VAL	Aren't you going to sit down . . . ?

(Silence.)

RICH   Do you think I should?

VAL   You look all tense stood up.

RICH   Aye, well . . .

(A beat.)

VAL   No chance of getting another brandy, is there?

(VAL holds out her glass. RICH pours her a drink, and pours himself one as well.)

VAL   Cheers!

RICH   There we go . . .

VAL   Bloody artist, then?

RICH   That's about it . . .

VAL   Never been in an artist's home before . . .

RICH   No?

VAL   What is it they say, are you going to show me your etchings?

(Silence.)

No, never been in an artist's house before. Been in a Chiropodist's.

RICH   Not the same, though!

VAL   Leo did one about seven months ago.

(VAL reclines.)

No, it's lovely in here . . . I've told him we need our house doing but he's that bloody busy . . . I mean it's all expense, isn't it?

RICH   That's right . . .

VAL   And it's so quiet, isn't it?

RICH	It'll not be if they start up!
VAL	Oh no, don't. I couldn't bear that, put me right off.
	(*A beat.*)
RICH	Funny job!
VAL	What's that?
RICH	That phone, erm . . .
VAL	Oh, it's nowt . . . I think too much emphasis on it. I mean sometimes, I only tell 'em my name and they're gone.
RICH	Gone?
VAL	Hung up . . .
RICH	That's right.
VAL	I mean I can put on a show on if they want one, but most of the time . . .
RICH	They're not that bothered?
VAL	It's money for old rope.
	(*A beat.*)
VAL	Well!
RICH	What?
VAL	Danny's gone . . .
RICH	He has . . .
	(*A beat.*)
VAL	So what do you think?
RICH	About what?
VAL	Well . . .

RICH   What?

VAL   Most men find me sexy.

         (*A beat.*)

RICH   So what are you saying?

VAL   What are you saying?

RICH   I'm saying, what are you saying?

VAL   I'm saying most men find me, you know . . .

RICH   Yeh well, I'm saying be careful . . .

VAL   Oh, right!

RICH   That's right.

VAL   Why's that, then?

RICH   You never know . . .

         (*A beat.*)

VAL   Why don't you come and sit here, then . . .

RICH   I might . . .

VAL   Why don't you?

RICH   I will when I'm ready!

VAL   I won't bite . . .

RICH   I might.

VAL   Well, I will if you want.

RICH   I'll think about it.

VAL   Come and sit down, and let's have a little chat.

         (RICH *goes and sits at the side of* VAL. *He is still quite tense about the situation. He nurses his drink.*)

Rich	Getting there!
	(*A beat.*)
Val	I'm not averse to anything as long as it doesn't hurt. Just tell me in advance though, I don't like surprises anymore!
Rich	Neither do I!
Val	I mean I had three once, years back now, but . . . and they were full of surprises!
Rich	No, three's never been a very good number for me!
	(*A beat.*)
Val	So do you want to kiss me, then?
Rich	Yes I do!
Val	Do you?
Rich	That's right!
Val	Oh . . . right then, Chuck . . .
	(Rich *stands.*)
Rich	Stand up . . .
Val	Oh, that game, is it?
	(Val *stands.*)
Rich	It's not a game . . .
Val	Do you think we need a bit of music on?
Rich	If you want . . .
	(Rich *walks over and reaches for the automatic console and clicks on a Piaf track. They both stand in silence as the music plays. They kiss tentatively, then he feels her hand.*)

VAL   Steady . . .

RICH   Come here . . .

             (*They start to kiss. It is soft to begin with and
             then it develops into a full passionate
             embrace.* RICH *grabs for* VAL'S *legs and tries to
             lift her off the floor, however she is far too
             generous for him to stand a fair chance.*)

VAL   Careful . . .

RICH   I want to . . .

VAL   Slow down a bit . . .

RICH   Come here . . .

             (RICH *attempts to hoist* VAL *once more. But
             gives out a yell, and puts her back down once
             more. And shakes his wrist.*)

RICH   Oh!

VAL   What's wrong?

RICH   Sprained my bloody wrist!

VAL   Careful!

RICH   Get back on the sofa . . . oh, my bloody wrist!

VAL   Calm down . . .

RICH   My bloody hand . . .

             (VAL *gets herself comfortable on the sofa.* RICH
             drops to his knees still nursing his wrist.)

VAL   Come on then . . .

RICH   (*holding his wrist*) Oh, hell!

VAL   Come on darlin' . . .

             (RICH *walks on his knees towards* VAL *but his
             knees are bad and he is agony as he makes his
             way towards her.*)

RICH	Oh, oh, oh!
VAL	What's wrong?
RICH	I've got arthritis in my knees!
VAL	Oh!
RICH	That dancing's not done them any good!
VAL	Let's go upstairs!
RICH	Hang on . . .
VAL	What?

(RICH *is struggling now to get to his feet. He cannot put weight onto his wrists, and cannot take the weight on his knees.*)

| RICH | I can't get up . . . |
| VAL | Are you all right? |

(RICH *is still on the floor and is struggling to get to his feet.*)

| RICH | Just give us a hand, will you? |

(VAL *helps him to his feet.*)

VAL	How's that?
RICH	Cheers.
VAL	Goor, you're after it, aren't you?
RICH	We'll go in the spare room.
VAL	Who sleeps there then?
RICH	Me . . . Becky sends me in there when I snore.
VAL	I hope you'll not be snoring tonight!

(RICH *kisses her.*)

| RICH | I mean I love her, but . . . |

VAL	Kiss me . . .
	(*He kisses her.*)
RICH	She's brilliant, but . . .
VAL	Kiss me.
	(*He kisses her.*)
RICH	Oh, my bloody wrist . . .
VAL	Shall I bring the brandy?
RICH	Bring what you want . . . oh, my bloody knees!
	(VAL *and* RICH *exit upstairs. The stage is empty. Only the plaintiff strains of Edith Piaf can be heard. Slowly and desolately* DANNY *enters with a can of beer and a piece of quiche. He munches on the quiche and looks around the room. He walks over to the music centre, Edith Piaf sings* Les Amants d'un Jour. *He stand and listens to the music, chewing on the quiche. As he does this quite enraptured by the music,* LEO *enters. He is silent, dangerous and unhappy.*)
DANNY	All rate?
LEO	(*exasperated*) Oh, Danny!
DANNY	What?
LEO	(*tired*) Oh dear . . .
DANNY	Go on then, get it out of your system! Because I know I'm going to hear it one day!
LEO	What?
DANNY	What happened?
LEO	Eh?
DANNY	What went off?
LEO	Oh, don't mate!

DANNY	Why not? Don't you usually swap notes?
LEO	No.
DANNY	So didn't she?
LEO	She comes off the bog, and we went into Sophie's room, she gets down on the bed, and the next thing you know . . .
DANNY	Don't, man . . .
LEO	She's heaving her guts up!
DANNY	Eh?
LEO	She's sick all over, all over the bed, the pillows, and then she sits up and sprays it all over the bedside rug.
DANNY	Oh, man!
LEO	What's she been eating?
DANNY	Just that hot dog!
LEO	Well that's what it is, then. It's all over the bloody bedroom.
DANNY	Bloody hell!
LEO	I've spent the last half-hour running a bath.
DANNY	What for?
LEO	To wash the rug out!
DANNY	Oh, man!
LEO	What else could I do? It's just floating there!
DANNY	Where is she?
LEO	Laid in a pillow full of spew . . .
DANNY	Oh, man . . .

LEO   I've been trying to change the bloody bed but I
            can't find any fucking sheets!

DANNY   So . . . nothing . . .

LEO   Nothing, absolute fucking zero, mate . . . So
            don't worry about it!

DANNY   Oh, man!

            (*A beat.*)

LEO   I told thee to watch her.

DANNY   I don't think she's had that much, to be
            honest!

LEO   Was she up for it?

DANNY   Well aye, but she obviously needed a drink.
            It's like me with flying . . .

            (*A beat.*)

LEO   So how did you get on, then?

DANNY   Eh?

LEO   With Val . . . ?

            (*A beat.*)

DANNY   Oh, well . . .

LEO   What?

DANNY   Had a refusal at Beeches . . .

LEO   You what?

DANNY   No man, I didn't . . . I mean . . .

LEO   Bloody good job then? 'Coz that would have
            been excellent, wouldn't it? Vicky throwing up
            all over me, and you getting all sorted out with
            Val. That would have gone down really well!

(*A beat.*)

DANNY   I dont think I'm cut out for this; not with my
         nerves. I mean, I've had to have an extra two of
         them diazepam tablets myself. I get all . . . you
         know that!

         (*A beat.*)

LEO   You didn't give any to Vicky, did you?

DANNY   What?

LEO   Did you give any of them tablets to Vicky?

         (*A beat.*)

DANNY   Well I just thought . . .

LEO   Oh, fucking excellent!

DANNY   She didn't know owt about it.

LEO   So she didn't want to?

DANNY   No, she did, but . . . I thought it might relax her.

LEO   So you didn't want her . . . ?

DANNY   Well no, I . . .

LEO   So we set this all up but you didn't want to?

DANNY   Well?

LEO   Very nice, mate.

DANNY   What can I –

LEO   Very nice! How many tablets did you give her?

DANNY   I gave her one, that's all.

LEO   Liar.

DANNY   I promise!

LEO   Liar!

DANNY   I erm . . .

LEO   How many tablets have you given her?

DANNY   Maybe three. It says on the bottle they make
             you drowsy . . . that's all. I –

LEO   Well they're not joking, are they?

             (*A beat.*)

             Danny, Danny, Danny! What are we going to
             do with you?

DANNY   I know.

             (*A beat.*)

LEO   So what shall we do now, then?

             (DANNY *eats his quiche.*)

DANNY   You don't want to fuck me, do you?

LEO   No!

DANNY   (*eating*) Do you want a piece of quiche then?
             Becky's made it.

LEO   I didn't come out tonight, Dan, expecting the
             climax of the evening to be a piece of home
             made bloody quiche . . . all right, mate? I had
             set my sights a little bit higher!

DANNY   She's got all these jams with different names
             on in the fridge, it's brilliant!

             (*A beat.*)

LEO   So where has Val got to, then?

DANNY   I dunno, she was talking to Nutty Norman
             when I went. She'd got this idea about the
             three of us getting started . . . but I thought
             well I don't really know her that well, and I've

only just met Nutty so I grabbed some snap and fucked off into the garden!

LEO   So has Val gone and . . . ?

DANNY   Listen, she was on about me watching . . .

LEO   So Val's gone with . . . ?

DANNY   (*eating*) I've no idea, mate.

LEO   Oh, Danny, Danny, Danny!

           (VAL *enters. She is adjusting herself.*)

VAL   What's up wi' you?

LEO   What's happening here?

VAL   How do you mean?

LEO   Well . . .

VAL   It's all worked out, hasn't it, cock?

LEO   Has it?

VAL   What?

LEO   Tell her . . .

VAL   What?

LEO   Vicky . . .

VAL   What about her?

LEO   Well, she's fast asleep in her own spew.

VAL   Well, she told me she –

LEO   Threw up and out like a light!

VAL   (*deducing*) So you . . . ?

LEO   Danny didn't like the idea, so –

DANNY   Hey, no!

LEO   I'm upstairs playing housemaid and
               presumably you and Rich have been getting
               sorted out! Which is just excellent!

VAL   Well how did I know?

               (LEO *starts to walk around the room.*)

LEO   Just brilliant, this is . . . It was my bloody idea
               and look at me!

VAL   Well how did anybody know, I mean me and
               Richard were just chatting, Danny had gone
               and . . . well . . .

LEO   But what has he brought to the bloody party,
               Val?

DANNY   (*eating*) Well like I say, this quiche is all right!

VAL   (*to* DANNY) Why didn't you say anything, you
               silly sod?

DANNY   Well, I didn't like, I didn't want to offend
               anybody!

LEO   No, that's right Danny, don't offend anybody
               for God's sake!

               (RICH *enters. He is looking rough and is coy.*
               LEO *and* RICH *look at each other. Silence.*)

VAL   (*coy*) All right?

RICH   (*slowly, almost silent*) Listen, I think there's
               been a mistake here . . .

LEO   Too fucking right there has!

RICH   A huge mistake . . .

LEO   That's right!

RICH   And I think you should go.

LEO	That's right!
RICH	Look, listen . . .
VAL	Leo, don't start . . .
LEO	Shut up a minute, you.
RICH	(*loudly*) I just think you should go!
LEO	You've had what you wanted, have you?
RICH	Now, listen, fair's fair!
LEO	Fair's fair, bloody hell?
RICH	Now eh, be reasonable.
LEO	Reasonable?
RICH	Hey, now look . . . Let's not –
LEO	Reasonable?
	(LEO *stands and confronts* RICH *who hands him off.*)
VAL	Leo, don't!
RICH	Look, I think you'd better go . . .
LEO	Don't touch me!
VAL	Leo? Leo . . . ?
LEO	Dont touch me or I'll eat you!
RICH	Look, I'm not having this!
LEO	You are . . .
RICH	I'm not having this in my own house.
	(RICH *storms out of the room.*)
LEO	(*to* DANNY) And you, you useless git!
VAL	Don't start shouting . . . I can't stand it . . .

(Leo *grabs* Val *around the face.*)

LEO   And you, you could have come and seen how
             anybody was getting on! But you're so full of
             your own thing, aren't you?

VAL   I thought you were getting sorted, so –

LEO   It's all self with you, isn't it?

DANNY   Don't take it out on Val.

LEO   Shut up you, you spineless git!

             (Rich *enters with a baseball bat and stands
             looking at them.*)

RICH   Right!

LEO   Oh, right . . . !

RICH   Right, come on then, let's get you sorted!

LEO   Think you're a bloody hard case, do you?

RICH   That's what it's all about, is it, with you lot?

VAL   Hey now, listen!

DANNY   Wow . . . hey, steady, don't do owt daft, man.

RICH   Think you can come in here and do what you
             want, do you?

LEO   I'll do you in a minute.

RICH   Will you?

LEO   I will.

RICH   (*shouts*) Come on then, you thick pig!

LEO   Grab him, Dan . . . We'll sort this bastard out!

             (Danny *makes a move.* Rich *hits him across the
             fingers and he is immediately incapacitated
             and falls to his knees.*)

DANNY	Arghhhh!
RICH	One down, two to go . . .
VAL	Hey listen, listen . . . !
DANNY	My fingers, he's broken my fuu . . .
RICH	(*to* LEO) Do you want some? Do you want some?
LEO	Hey, hey, hey . . . !
VAL	Now come on, we're all adults . . .
DANNY	(*crying in agony*) My foooo . . .
VAL	We're all adults chuck, aren't we?
RICH	Are we?
LEO	Bloody hell, calm down!
RICH	Aye, we're all adults so let's stop the remarks, shall we?
LEO	What remarks?
RICH	Oh, come on . . .
LEO	What are you on about?
RICH	Let's leave off talking about my wife and daughter, shall we?
LEO	(*shouting*) Well, that's rich because you've just shagged mine!
	(DANNY *is rolling in agony.*)
DANNY	Oh, my fooooo . . .
RICH	I have, and shall I tell you what it took?
LEO	Hey, it's just a joke . . .
VAL	Everybody's had a drink, everybody's gone a bit too far!

LEO	It's been a good night, hasn't it? It's been a good night!
RICH	She was six bottles of Pils, two glasses of red wine and three brandys!
LEO	Hey, listen . . .
RICH	That's what it took.
LEO	Hey. Hey . . .
RICH	Oh, and a bowl of chicken and mushroom soup! Not a very good score!
VAL	Hey now, we're all adults, kid, so –
RICH	Of course we're all adults.
VAL	We're all adults.
LEO	Course we are, no problem . . .
RICH	Well, when this adult tells you to turn the fuckin' music down, turn it down!
LEO	What?
RICH	Turn it down . . .
LEO	Fair enough!
RICH	What will Sophie be doing tonight?
VAL	Eh?
RICH	I'm not being offensive, am I?
LEO	What are you on about?
RICH	You know what I'm on about!
DANNY	(*agony*) My bloody hand!
LEO	Wow, hey . . . you're a mile off!

(DANNY *is sat nursing his fingers.*)

DANNY	Tha's broken my hand, you arse. Oh!
RICH	Am I?
LEO	A bloody mile off.
RICH	You've done nothing in here, it's taken you all day and you haven't got one wall ready, all you've done is make snide remarks about me and my family, you cunts!
LEO	Wow, steady . . . now steady with the language.
RICH	Just get out!
LEO	We're going . . .
RICH	Get out!
DANNY	We've to get Vicky . . . she's in Sophie's room, so –
RICH	Better go and get her!
VAL	Come on Dan, I'll come with you. (*To* RICH.) Bloody hell Rich, you know how to spoil a party.
RICH	I do, don't I?
	(VAL *and* DANNY *exit*. LEO *and* RICH *stand in silence. They are looking at each other.* RICH *picks up the video and offers it to* LEO.)
LEO	Bloody hell?
RICH	Yes?
LEO	Bloody hell . . .
RICH	Yes?
LEO	And I thought that tha' wa' an all right bloke . . .
RICH	Well you were wrong there, weren't you?

LEO	It's no big deal . . . don't worry about it.
RICH	Don't you worry about it!
LEO	You've gone over the line, mate.
RICH	Do you think so?
LEO	You've gone too far!
RICH	Yeh?
LEO	You're a bloody animal . . . !
RICH	Well it takes one to know one.
LEO	They need the police around here, you want fuckin' locking up!
RICH	Get out.

(LEO *exits.* RICH *follows him upstage and off stage. Silence.* RICH *returns he is sweating tired, half-drunk and frightened. He starts to piece together some of the things in his living room. He looks at the photo of* BECKY *from Puerto Banus. As he does* SOPHIE *enters.*)

SOPHIE	Have you seen these out here?
RICH	What . . . ?
SOPHIE	What's been going on?
RICH	Eh?
SOPHIE	Have you had those people around?
RICH	Who?
SOPHIE	Bill and Ben and whoever they're with?
RICH	Oh, go to bed!
SOPHIE	Have those two women been –
RICH	(*shouting*) I said go to bed, all right?

SOPHIE	Have they been in here?
RICH	Yes, they have!
SOPHIE	Have they been smoking?
RICH	Amongst other things yes, they've been smoking!
SOPHIE	We don't want them around here, do we?
RICH	Why not, they're only people aren't they? What are you . . . scared of becoming one of them?
SOPHIE	They're as common as muck.
RICH	Says who?
SOPHIE	Just look at them.
RICH	(*strongly*) Go to bed, love.
SOPHIE	What have you been doing, though?
RICH	Go to bed!
SOPHIE	Wait till I tell Mum, she'll go mad!
	(SOPHIE *moves off stage very quickly.*)
RICH	(*to himself*) She will, won't she?
	(*Silence.* RICH *soaks in his guilt.* SOPHIE *enters with soiled sheets.*)
SOPHIE	And what's all this?
RICH	That's vomit, Sophie. That's what that is.
	(*Music. Blackout.*)

Scene Four

The lounge. 9.00 am.

DANNY and LEO *enter, they have their CD player with them.*
They act almost as if nothing has happened, and begin to tidy
around in the lounge. DANNY *has his hand heavily bandaged*
and can only work with one arm. They begin to put dust sheets
over the furniture.

LEO	We'll get in here ready, shall we?
DANNY	Can do!
	(DANNY *sees the video on the floor.*)
	Do you want this video?
LEO	Aye, can do . . .
DANNY	Be a laugh . . .
LEO	Put it in my bag . . . We'll have a look at that. After.
	(RICH *enters. He is clearly badly hungover. He looks at* DANNY *and* LEO. LEO *switches off the music.*)
	What's up now?
RICH	Bloody hell!
LEO	What?
RICH	What are you doing?
LEO	There's a job to do, isn't there . . . ?
	(*A beat.*)
RICH	Bloody hell . . .
LEO	Right Danny, let's crack on, mate.
DANNY	Sophie's back, then?
RICH	That's right . . .
DANNY	She have a good night?

RICH   You'll have to ask her, we're not talking . . .

            (*A beat.*)

LEO   Any chance of getting a cuppa then, mate . . . ?

            (*Silence.*)

RICH   (*slowly*) No milk, four sugars and a Kit Kat?

LEO   It's a start.

DANNY   Mars bar for me . . .

RICH   Right.

LEO   Right, then!

DANNY   Cheers.

            (*A beat.*)

RICH   I'll put the kettle on then, shall I?

LEO   That'd be good!

            (RICH *exits. Silence.*)

DANNY   So what do you think?

LEO   About what?

DANNY   About last night?

LEO   (*innocent*) What about it?

DANNY   (*dead*) That's right.

            (*A beat.*)

LEO   How was Vicky this morning, then?

DANNY   A bit rough. Why?

LEO   Ar . . . well . . .

DANNY   What?

LEO	Maybe it was a bit too close to home anyway.
DANNY	Do you reckon?
LEO	Pity, though.
DANNY	Why?
LEO	Your lass, man.
DANNY	What?
LEO	It's all natural isn't it?

(BECKY *appears at the doorway.*)

BECKY	Oh, in here now, are you?
LEO	Making a start.
BECKY	You get all over, don't you?
LEO	We will do, don't fret about that!
DANNY	Back early, then?
BECKY	Oh, dear.
LEO	Yeah?
BECKY	What a night!
DANNY	Oh, lovely . . .
BECKY	Never again.
DANNY	That's what they all say.
LEO	One of those nights, was it?
BECKY	I'm afraid so, I came away at one, stayed over in Nottingham.
LEO	Party pooper, eh?
BECKY	Well everyone was legless by then and trying to get into bed with each other.

DANNY	Pathetic, isn't it?
BECKY	It's not pretty, I can assure you; a load of forty-somethings thinking they're eighteen!
LEO	Not for you, then?
BECKY	Not for me!
LEO	Oh, right . . .
BECKY	Why?
LEO	That's a pity.
BECKY	Is it?
LEO	Well, don't they say that variety is the spice –
BECKY	(*tense*) They say a lot of things.
LEO	(*loaded*) They do, don't they?
	(*A beat.*)
BECKY	So how are we doing here?
LEO	Oh . . . all the stairs needs re-plastering, and the guest room's ceiling is a mess. I mean it could be an eight week job . . .
BECKY	Really?
LEO	Oh, aye . . . it's going to be more complicated than we thought, isn't it Dan?
DANNY	Aye, it's turning out to be a right nightmare . . .
	(RICH *enters, with a tray with biscuits and two mugs of tea, and a Mars bar.*)
RICH	Back early, aren't you?
BECKY	Can you smell smoke in here?
RICH	Me?

LEO	Aye that's me, sorry, must have brought the smell in with me.
RICH	So how did you get on?
BECKY	Oh, unbelievable . . .
RICH	Yeh?
BECKY	A nightmare, the whole sad bunch . . .
RICH	Well, there you go . . . Right here you are, tea lads . . .
LEO	Cheers, mate.
DANNY	Smashing . . .
	(DANNY *and* LEO *grab their respective cups.*)
BECKY	So what do you get up to?
RICH	Oh, I . . .
	(*A beat.*)
LEO	Just went for a Chinese, didn't you?
RICH	That's about it.
BECKY	I knew he wouldn't stay in!
RICH	Well you can't stay in on a Friday, can you?
DANNY	It's hard, isn't it?
LEO	I was just saying to Becks though, Rich, it's gonna take us longer than we thought.
RICH	Aye, I thought it might.
BECKY	Is Sophie up yet? I'll leave you to it, shall I?
	(BECKY *exits. Silence.*)

LEO   We'd better get on with it then, hadn't we?

RICH   That's right.

DANNY   A good night, wasn't it?

RICH   Was it?

LEO   Oh aye, a good night . . .

               (*A beat.*)

RICH   I've had better . . .

               (*A beat.*)

LEO   Aye, that's what Val said. Turn the music on
               Dan.

               (DANNY *switches on the music.* LEO *looks at*
               RICH. *Milly Jackson's 'My Man A Sweet Man'*
               plays. DANNY *and* LEO *begin to prepare the*
               walls. RICH *watches them and then begins to*
               help. Music swells as the lights fade to
               blackout.)